Bindy's
Moon

Bindy's
Moon

LLOYD RATZLAFF

thistledown press

Thistledown Press Ltd.
410 2nd Avenue North
Saskatoon, Saskatchewan, S7K 2C3
www.thistledownpress.com

Library and Archives Canada Cataloguing in Publication

Ratzlaff, Lloyd, 1946–, author
Bindy's moon / Lloyd Ratzlaff.
Essays.
Issued in print and electronic formats.
ISBN 978-1-77187-054-2 (pbk.).–ISBN 978-1-77187-070-2 (html).–
ISBN 978-1-77187-071-9 (pdf)

I. Title.
PS8585.A853B56 2015   C818'.603   C2015-900485-3
C2015-900486-1

Author photo by Larraine Ratzlaff
Cover and book design by Jackie Forrie
Printed and bound in Canada

Canada Council for the Arts   Conseil des Arts du Canada   SASKATCHEWAN ARTS BOARD   Canadian Heritage   Patrimoine canadien

Thistledown Press gratefully acknowledges the financial assistance of the Canada Council for the Arts, the Saskatchewan Arts Board, and the Government of Canada through the Canada Book Fund for its publishing program.

In memory of Jim
1944 – 1998

The events of childhood do not pass, they return like seasons of
the year. — Eleanor Farjeon

After dinner I by water alone to Westminster, towards the parish church, and met with Mr. Howlett, who, offering me a pew in the gallery, I had no excuse but up with him I must go, and then much against my will staid out the whole church, but I did entertain myself with my perspective glass up and down the church, by which I had the great pleasure of gazing at a great many very fine women; and what with that and sleeping, I passed away the time till sermon was done.

— *The Diary of Samuel Pepys*, May 26, 1666

Once I looked at the moon and caught sight of a strange thing. A cricket had perched upon the handrail, only a few inches away from me. My line of vision was such that the creature filled the moon like a fossil. It had gone there, I thought, to live and die, for there, of all places, was its small definition made whole and eternal. A warm wind rose up and purled like the longing within me.

— N. Scott Momaday, *The Way to Rainy Mountain*

Proem

OUTGROWING AN OLD MYTHOLOGY INTELLECTUALLY is a first (and in hindsight relatively easy) step. Bearing its emotional freight is another matter. The "Bindy" for whom this book is named grew up with me speaking a religiously fundamentalist and ethnically Mennonite tongue. Despite its anathemas, or because of them, this language became a strop on which our thoughts were keened — for Bindy until he died and for me to this day.

Arthur Miller calls writing a way of synthesizing all of one's insides. This book is a sort of philosophical tussle with Blake's old Nobodaddy throughout the year of Bindy's dying. Partly it's a confession (a scary bipolar genre, scorned at the newsstand and extolled in St. Augustine), but also, perhaps, a kind of repentance of my former uses of language in wordy careers as a minister, counsellor, and university instructor.

"At night," Rumi says, "I open the window and ask the moon to come and press its face against mine. Breathe into me . . . Close the language-door and open the love-window, the moon won't use the door, only the window."

Winter

Lamp in a Gloom

Bindy, I fear you're fading. You seem to have lost the battle, and what will I do when you die?

Bindy: this name from your infancy, when your parents introduced you to our half-deaf grandfather as Jimmy, and he heard Bindy, and the nickname stuck. You pointed at the moon (your mother says always with a middle finger) crying *Kahnee-kah, kahnee-kah*, a childish German for *Kann ich haben* — why, why can't I have it?

Now it seems you're groping back toward a fundamentalism I thought we had both outgrown. I'd still like to wring that religion's neck, roast and eat the fowl, and pull apart the wishbone.

☾

A dream:

Deep in a winter night at the farm where Jim grew up, and where our fathers had grown up before him. I sit in a folding chair in the yard, peering around the back end of a truck to discover the source of the light that casts this marvellous glow on the snowdrifts all around. And I see it comes from a yard light at a farm across the north field.

It seems I am reliving a very old and deep experience, something from childhood which I had long forgotten. But this ecstasy — how can it be contained?

I pick up my chair and carry it over the drifts, past the barn and out to the lane, and sit again listening for sounds from the east pasture and the dugout.

Behind me in the farmhouse, others are fast asleep. Out here there is only silence, and this abiding rapture I know has always been in me though I haven't felt it in a long while, and a deep certainty that all childhood is intact.

Our fathers were the second and third siblings of seven brothers and one sister (four other girls had died in childhood, three of them within a year), and our mothers are youngest sisters in their family of nine. Jim is a bit older than I, and with no biological brothers of my own I've always regarded him as both soul-brother and spiritual kin.

He's a mechanical wizard (pronouncing the word *mechennical,* in true Mennonite form) who's worked for twenty-five years as an electronics technician with plasma physics researchers at the University of Saskatchewan. Fifteen years ago I resigned as a minister of the Mennonite church, and since then have worked on the campus as a sessional lecturer in educational psychology. Jim likes to introduce us as double cousins (and often adds, "He's teaching teachers," while I think, *Every day Jim gets to discuss philosophy with scientists*). His colleagues like to quote his line: "If it doesn't smoke or make noise, I don't want it." Or they lampoon him: if their nuclear fusion experiments fail, it's because the tokomak is "contaminated with Jimium."

Two years ago Bindy (how affectionate the name feels now) was diagnosed with encephalitis, but this medical "through-knowing" — *dia gnosis* — proved to be ignorant of a malignant brain tumour. When it was discovered he took the recommended radiation and chemotherapy, travelled at his own expense to the Mayo Clinic in Rochester, and came home with holes in his head from a clumsy apparatus more primitive, he said, than equipment he himself built for the university. And though he had some months of reprieve, the cancer was back just before his fifty-fourth birthday, more ferocious than before. Everyone had urged him to try another round of treatments, which he's undergoing now, but he phrased the decision as a majority vote, wondering himself whether it's not "time to fold the tent."

((

January on the Canadian prairie is a two-faced god with seasonal affective disorder, one side dark as the devil and the other pining for a crocus on bare ground. Cold lies heavy on life and earth. Sol labours from horizon to horizon but every day runs out of light early.

The CBC's financial analyst says bonds are the way to go, at least for the first part of the year, depending on what happens with inflation. He fears a recession: the economy must grow — no matter that it's from a million warbling widgets, only that everything grows and grows, every tumour benign and happy.

In my discipline of psychology, professors today will instruct students in testing, measuring, and slotting — recommend maybe this, maybe that, for anyone who doesn't fall under acceptable regions of the bell curve.

Larraine, my wife, teaches English as an Alternate Language to immigrant students, and last night she dreamt of a moon shifting shape from round to irregular and printing out a message: *YOU IDIOT!* She's dealing with painful symptoms which her doctor attributes to shingles. He's surprised they haven't broken out more fully, and says they probably come of her being "worn out."

Our good friends Brent and Ellen live in the apartment above. Brent works for Air Canada, and just before Christmas smashed his knee falling to the tarmac from the belly of a jet while unloading cargo. He knew back in high school that his main aim in life was to see the world beyond the Miramichi, where he grew up in New Brunswick. First he became a travel agent, then an airline employee, and now often says with gusto, "The world is my oyster." Between company passes and shift-trades, and with Ellen's part-time work at the public library, they've been accustomed to flying around the world for a week, or a month, and coming back with stories to make their friends envy. Now he languishes in Royal University Hospital with round-the-clock care, promising (or threatening) to live even harder when he recovers.

Today Brent's physicians, like Jim's, will work longer hours than most of the rest of us; they may be among the most stressed people on earth as they save other lives while staving off death-thoughts of their own.

And Bindy, ah my brother, I fear he's on the verge of a great transformation.

☾

Miss Biliske, my third grade teacher, had led us through stiff wind and drifting snow from the Laird School to the community hall for a dress rehearsal for the evening's Christmas concert. The back of the hall was chilly when we arrived, but near the front a pot-bellied stove burned red-hot, and by the time we'd hung up our parkas and been seated on wooden planks below the stage, the place was sweltering.

The principal, Mr. Bergen, had brought his senior students earlier. Old Simon (as we called him behind his back) was short and he walked with a limp, but his arms were thick and he had a voice like a bull, and we all sat waiting on the benches, mostly behaving ourselves.

As other classes arrived, I remembered an assembly in the school hallway a few weeks before, when an older kid nicknamed Pluto had fainted. He was a head taller than the principal, but Old Simon hoisted him from the floor and slung him over a shoulder and hauled him away gimping — we saw how Pluto's arms dangled and swayed, and I was sure he was dead.

Later the teacher said he had only fainted from standing too long in the heat, but I was certain he must have come very near death, and even at the age of nine knew what kind of heat there'd be for some people — possibly me — after they died and landed in hell.

The principal whistled for attention and outlined procedures for the rehearsal. Miss Biliske led our class to a small staircase and up through the wing, and lined us in a row at the front of the stage. Other classes came through the opposite wing and stood behind us, and by now I was thinking, *What if it's me who faints this time, what if I have to be carried out? And if I die — what then?*

Another teacher began unpacking a large cardboard box full of gifts and arranging them under the tree. Mr. Bergen dragged a table from the wall and pushed it against the stage and set a chair on top of it. He warned us not to horse around, then hopped up to the table and climbed on the chair, glowering at us kids in front, it seemed, and looking eye-to-eye at those in the back. For an instant I wondered how he'd conduct songs without falling off that rickety perch, but he raised his baton and the piano played an introduction, and we began singing, *Joy to the world! the Lord is come.*

Sure enough, within a few minutes a girl in the next row keeled over. Bergen leaped from his chair onto the stage and lifted her, carried her through the wing and downstairs and out the door while her teacher followed close behind. Now I was in a panic — two people down, not everyone will wake up like Pluto did, like this girl might, and hell is hotter by far than the community hall.

When the principal returned he only said, "Don't worry about her, she'll be all right. Now we'll rehearse the next number." But I waved for Miss Biliske to come, and blurted out, "I don't feel too good." She went to get a male teacher, who came and lifted me by the armpits and swung me down onto a bench right beside the stove, which still cast its terrible heat, but already now my faintness seemed to be passing.

For the next hour I sat listening to carols, watching others perform skits and recite poems. The girl who had fainted was back and sitting on a bench nearby, seemingly no worse for the experience. But later as I trudged home through the snow, I felt ashamed of my faint-heartedness.

That night when my parents and I returned to the hall all dressed up for the show, the place only seemed warm and pleasant. I took my seat near the Christmas tree, which stood glowing in the corner with its crown nearly touching the ceiling and branches sheltering a great circle of gifts.

A few minutes before the concert began, Sheila Code, who was a year older than I, stood up and turned the backs of her legs to a friend and asked, "Are the seams of my nylons straight?" And the scent of pine and candles mingled with a dim stirring of passion, the community hall was packed to the doors, our teachers led us onstage, Old Simon mounted his rostrum, and we all sang, *Dashing through the snow in a one-horse open sleigh, ho-ho.*

The concert passed without rowdiness, the principal's scaffold did not collapse, no one fainted, the audience whistled and cheered. Then came the Jolly Man who handed me a gift. I tore it open, and there Joan Dyck had given me *The Adventures of Tom Sawyer*, exactly what I had wanted. Ushers delivered paper bags with peanuts and hard striped candies and a single Japanese orange — who could die now, with the world so full of joy?

(

One Christmas my daughter Shannon and her husband Ramsy came to visit for the holidays from the Okanagan Valley. She and her younger sister Sheri had been on the verge of adolescence when their mother and I parted, and after that every Christmas felt empty, as if someone was not at home, and that someone was me. Not until I met my new partner Larraine did I feel a requickening of the holiday spirit, for in every festive season she turned into an exuberant child, and her joy was contagious.

That Christmas Eve as we began exchanging gifts, Shannon said the smallest package under the tree should be opened last. When we got to it, Larraine and I unwrapped a tiny picture frame without a photo, but underneath the glass it held a note that read, *To Grandpa and Memé,* with a date in the summer when their first child was expected. This little frame, devoid of image but so full of promise, made that Christmas merry indeed.

The following week, after a New Year's Eve dinner, Shannon said, "Dad, let's go for a walk, just you and me." We bundled up and headed along St. Henry Avenue, and at the first lamppost she stepped into the circle of light at our feet, turned to face me and said, "Dad, whatever you think you've done wrong, I forgive you."

The night had brightened again. We hugged each other and continued walking past the street lamps to the far end of St. Henry, where the railway tracks run by a clump of trees and a snowdrift had formed. Shannon flopped face down into it and waggled her limbs. I fell beside her on my back and flapped mine, and when we got up she pointed at the small depression left in the snow by her stomach and said, "There's your grandchild."

☾

Brent's knee surgery has been delayed because of still-unexplained "complications." Meanwhile, this evening in his hospital room a nasty-looking machine was working his leg over — hoisting, pulling, rotating — and only the regular shots of morphine made his pain bearable and somewhat tempered his impatience to get on with life.

Late at night, Ellen and Larraine and I left through an old wing of the hospital. Rounding a corner in the hallway, we nearly collided with a velvet-draped gurney being wheeled head and foot toward the elevator by two silent morticians.

Dear Shannon, Dear Sheri,

A midnight letter from Dad. The apartment is quiet, though sometimes I hear Larraine cough in the bedroom or Ellen walking around upstairs, probably anxious for Brent. Otherwise it's only the sounds of my pen scratching the paper, and puffs I make on my pipe.

I hope you're happy in your marriages. I'm very fond of Ramsy and Rob, and promise never to interfere with your relationships or be anything but an ally to all of you.

I'm sure you know that underneath my anger at your mother it was all sorrow — sorrow that our love didn't hold and that you had to grow up among our insecurities. But in spite of our failures, you are graces I can hardly fathom, and never a day passes that I'm not grateful for all you've become.

Thank you. I love you.

((

Jim had sounded alert on the phone, but when I got to his house he was sitting vacantly on the couch as the TV played in the background. Our visit fell flat. When he did talk, it was mostly about an upcoming EEG and of having to surrender his driver's license. He wants to interrogate the doctors, he said, about why he "can't drive car no more."

Soon he lay down facing the tube, half turning his back to me. I sat beside him on the floor, wanting to be close even though I had no idea what to say. Laura, his wife, stayed busy in the kitchen, and it was a relief when their nine-year-old Dustin got home and began reporting on his school day.

Jim says he hates the thought of losing a parental role with Dusty, as he did with Julie, their daughter who died at the age of thirteen from Reye's syndrome and a medical blunder that must have been nearly impossible to forgive. He never seemed to recover from that tragedy; today I couldn't see a response from him even when Dusty tried to snuggle with his dad on the couch.

A mutual friend called and asked to come over. When he arrived, Jim sat up and talked about his cancer, but soon the conversation turned to hunting and snowmobiling — two passions they've long shared — and for a time Jim became quite animated. When he lay down again, Dusty went to his room and Jim was facing the other friend.

Dear brother — same mythology in our genes, same relatives as role models, same guilts in our souls. I wasn't sure you wanted me there today.

☾

Hotei, a laughing Buddha, stands in a nook between two bookshelves in our living room. A broad-bellied, wide-grinning, robed and embeaded little man, he hoists a boat over his head, and in the boat a globe of light that drives the darkness from our room and lifts up our hearts. This is no Buddha to sit absorbed in nirvana — he leaves the Enlightened One under the bo tree while himself carrying a gleam through the world, all the way into our living room. Hefting that load straightens his spine and forgives the fat belly, but *oy,* what a crick he must have in his back.

Even so, catch him unsmiling if you can.

Hotei doesn't mind whether I switch him on or keep groping in my dark; he upholds the globe — lit, unlit — and never seems to weary of serving up a smile. Every morning he sends me into the world without forbidding me to take my way, and at night shows me what to come home to.

I salute you, sir. I vow to heft and to smile.

One year at a writing retreat I pulled aside a bed in my room to rearrange furniture, and a gnarled manikin lay looking up at me from the floor. He was a twig with a hole in one side, back humped like a knuckle, right leg stunted and the left hacked off, his two jagged arms imploring heaven and earth.

Sometimes now it seems that for all his grotesquerie, he might stand on his head more easily than Hotei with his belly-laughs.

I salute you, gnarled man, and vow to bear my own beggarliness.

((

Jim and I grew up in a rural, poverty-ridden, ethnic fundamentalism that cajoled us into premature responsibilities, with precious few graces for the inevitable eruptions of our repressed spirit, sex, and art. We came into the world hungry but culturally retarded — not necessarily incapacious, but forever tardy hobbledehoys.

Our life was dominated by God the father, Christ his only begotten son, and an arcane spirit said to bring the other two into this world from their remote heavenly home. How God could have a son with no woman in his heaven was a conundrum for theologians to explain, but our church itself was less a mother than a righteous bitch threatening with hellfire to keep us on a straight track to heaven. We were fed stories of a "substitutionary atonement" in which the obedient son had satisfied the bloodthirsty father (no forgiveness without bloodshed!), and if only we believed this right it would guarantee salvation, and someday we'd leave this world of sin and sweat and enter heaven with personalities cleansed and bodies made new.

The ills and complexes of such unfeminine religion put the fear of God into us without knowing how to remove it, and we lived in fear of Man, Woman, Nature, Devil, and especially God. Love was both commanded and forbidden, with sex the culprit at the boundary throttling our capacity to love or feel loved, though the scriptures promised that "perfect love casts out fear." Forgiveness was hardly more than a grudging probation without power to transform life, and led mainly to a pseudo-spirituality in which (to alter the old proverb) an ounce of pretension was worth a pound of manure.

We didn't know what to do with this flawed deity who rejected his own creation, being so holy (it was said) that he couldn't bear to look upon our sins, and his need to punish must at all costs be satisfied. By our fear and servility we kept nursing this God bent on damning us, and our pastors and teachers seemed to do the same. We became infected with his self-righteousness while claiming nonetheless to be "saved by grace, and not by works, lest any man should boast."

☾

My father never got beyond elementary school. He stayed to work on the family farm while his six brothers and one surviving sister went away to Bible institutions to acquire an education that seemed to make him feel inferior for much of his life, though he may well have been the most inventive of them all. Once in a while he allowed himself to joke about "higher learning" — like the guy who got his BS degree and then also a PhD, bullshit piled higher and deeper.

In my early years as a minister I once attended a retreat where we were asked to reflect on our childhoods. I remembered something my father had done when I was nine years old, and wrote him a letter of thanks. By then I already suspected that the lack of his siblings' kind of education only meant he didn't have quite as much bullshit to unlearn.

He replied with a note of his own, written in blunt pencil on a ruled page. He said he remembered the incident only vaguely, but thanked me for writing, and before signing off added, "I was very tuched by your letter."

My third grade teacher had planned to stage a play that called for one little character to walk on crutches. She soon discovered that no one owned a pair to fit an eight-year-old, and asked whether someone's father might be able to build them. I knew that my dad was handy, and said so. But crutches! — wouldn't these have to be bought in some kind of store?

Miss Biliske asked me to call home. I climbed the narrow staircase to old Bergen's office and pulled his chair to where the school's only telephone hung on the wall, climbed up and cranked our ring, *long-short-long*. My mother answered, and went to get Dad from the workshop. He listened to my request and said he'd try to make the crutches.

One reason I thought he just might be able to do this was that he'd already built a go-kart for me. We called it a "tractor" because the bicycle wheels on the back were tall, like a tractor's, and the smaller front wheels had been salvaged from a Radio Flyer wagon Dad had found at the "junk pile," our term for the dump a mile northeast of town. My tractor had a real gasoline engine which had once powered a washing machine in our porch, as well as a wooden dashboard with a real ignition switch and throttle and a nonfunctional temperature gauge Dad had rescued from some abandoned car. The steering wheel was fashioned from a thick metal rod he had bent in a circle and welded together.

Often I took an empty floorwax tin and one of my precious dimes to George Klassen's garage up the street. He'd pump the handle of his bowser a few times and drain ten cents' worth of amber gas through the spout into my can. Back home I filled the tractor tank — another wax tin soldered to the engine by a copper line — flipped the toggle on the dash, stomped on the pedal until the motor chugged into life, and took my seat between the back wheels, which came to shoulder height and had no fenders to protect fingers from spokes.

I pushed the hand clutch forward and the tractor lurched into motion. I opened the throttle and tore around the yard, into the back alley, through the yard again, and up the street as far as the Imperial Bank, where I turned in a tight arc (the tractor had no reverse gear) and headed home again through dust I had raised.

This machine was the envy of my peers. Even older kids begged and bribed me to let them drive it, the petitions coming in such numbers that I had to begin charging fees to recover the cost of my gas. One day Grant Peters, a rich neighbour, offered to trade a stack of comics for the tractor — "a stack this high," he said, with a gesture that to me represented many hundreds of them. He never knew that in my family comic books were forbidden, and that his offer had actually tempted me at first.

I soon grew confident in driving, with only a few mishaps, but other kids fared less well. They drove headlong into tight corners and dead ends, butted the tractor's nose against fences with the back wheels churning until the engine sputtered out; or they came charging at spectators and nearly crashed into them before veering aside, so that before long Dad had to gear down the axle and greatly temper the thrills of speed, and build tin fenders to shield the back wheels.

Strange that amid this heady popularity I still envied Bev Hinz. He owned a shiny orange pedal tractor bought from the Rosthern Macleod's store, and to me it was a beautiful thing. Bev coveted my tractor as much as I did his, so we struck up an accord: he'd drive mine, I'd drive his, and both of us were sure we'd gotten the better deal.

By the time I neared my teens, Dad had also found two abandoned bicycles at the junk pile, and from their frames and wheels and fenders built what looked like a hybrid between a boy's and girl's bike. Its crossbars sloped down at peculiar angles, and Dad's jagged weldseams quickly began to rust. If I ever parked my bike in the schoolyard beside the high-priced units others drove, I felt almost as ashamed of it as I had once been proud of the tractor, which by this time I'd outgrown.

That day in grade three when I phoned home, somewhere around mid-afternoon Dad delivered a pair of crutches to the school. Too modest to appear at the classroom door himself, he called ahead to say he'd leave them in a corner at the school's entrance. Miss Biliske sent me out to fetch them, and there they stood against the wall, the perfect height for a third grade player to hobble around the stage of Laird Community Hall, and so finely built that to me they looked as good as any to be had from a store.

And wasn't the teacher overjoyed — now the play would go on.

☾

Larraine and I were preparing dinner and catching up on the day when she pointed distractedly at some rust spots on the bottom of the cast iron frying pan. I assumed she was showing me that I hadn't done a very good job of dishwashing, a task that normally falls to me in our domestic division of labour.

For the previous three days a broom had been standing beside a pile of dust in one corner of the kitchen, which she had left there herself — it's one of her (to me) inscrutable penchants — and all I saw was the similarity between her half-sweeping and my half-assed washing. How often she's urged me to make jokes about things that irritate me, and for once I thought I was doing so when I said, "Funny how that frying pan is a bit like your dust pile in the corner."

I saw she was stung. After a long silence I asked whether she was upset. She denied it, but went to lie on the couch while I continued cooking, fretting now at how my good intentions had backfired, until finally I went to explain.

It turned out that she had washed the frying pan herself, failing to clean it to her own standards, and she'd had no idea what my remark meant. I had attempted the biblical absurdity of removing a speck of sawdust from her eye when there was a sizable plank in my own.

We had just finished eating when Laura called in a last-minute search for someone to sit with Jim while she took Dusty to a track meet at the Saskatoon Field House. I was glad to spend some time alone with my brother who so intimately knows our past, its rural roots and urban longings. When I got there he had birch logs burning in the basement fireplace, but lay on the couch under a blanket apparently angry that he wasn't allowed to accompany his family or to stay home alone, and he resented being babysat.

Dusty was nervous about his race, but when they left Jim didn't so much as wish him good luck, and as soon as the door closed he asked, "Would you like to watch one of my gospel music videos?"

"Sure, Jim," I said, "I'd like to do whatever you want." And I did want to follow his lead, but had hoped for another fireside chat like so many we'd had before. But he wanted only to lie under a blanket and watch these southern Bible-belt singers raising hands and shouting *Glory*, or weeping and praying down the spirit. Once in a while he'd say, "That's the bass singer from the Cathedrals . . . That's Vestal Goodman . . . That's Jake Hess — he's survived every disease known to man" (cancer, bad heart, and several other ailments which Jim recited).

In three hours of this, hardly anything else was said. Occasionally he mentioned how close to death some of the singers appeared. Sometimes I'd make a comment about a group I remembered from childhood — then he'd start from his pillow, and I knew I had disturbed his sleep.

When Laura and Dusty got home I asked how things had gone. Dusty said, "We came in second-last." Jim mumbled from the couch, "Well, *some*body has to be last," and the kid protested, "But we weren't *last!*"

Often Jim says Dusty is his main reason for living.

Laura stood in her coat at the foot of the stairs. "It's late. Dusty didn't run till 9:30. Maybe you should stop this now. I have to take you to your chemo tomorrow."

Eventually he sat up, but his eyes stayed fixed on the screen and he was still watching the singers when I left.

At home I made love to Larraine. There was no sex, but I saw her, I hoped, with eyes from which a few scales had fallen.

☾

At the gates of Wanuskewin, a First Nations heritage park at the fringe of Saskatoon, a group of bronze sculptures by Lloyd Pinay draws me in.

A sinuous woman waves a ragged deerskin flap over her head to deflect three running bison — bull, cow, and calf — toward a crouching brave in horned headdress who lures the beasts toward the river bank where their animal ancestors once tumbled into the ravine below.

Bronze hair falls to her waist, her slender body is wrapped in a deerskin garment crossed discreetly over her breasts, deerhide moccasins raise her on tiptoe vigilance.

For an instant I'm frightened as I peer into her eyes — how she sees through me, who can scarcely be in her world — and suddenly shy to view the rest of the sculpted body which on other visits has seemed so erotic.

I circle the sculptures. The eros has gone, but the eyes keep looking through.

☾

We call them Becky's bells, but really they're wind chimes our niece made for us one year from a bag of mismatched cutlery she bought at the Sally Ann.

Suspended from the fireplace mantel, curving down like a swan's neck, is the handle of a kitchen fork with tines bent in four directions and curlicue flourishes at their ends; and hung from the tines on bright-beaded threads are a tarnished butter knife and three sizes of kitchen spoons.

On winter nights Larraine and I light a fire, and as the air begins to circulate and the room to warm, Becky's bells sound. First, a single note *faint as the bells of sleep.* Then two utensils ringing together, each in its own tone — *Te Deum*, and presently all four twirl and jangle happily in concert, and I begin to name my graces.

Oak bookshelves built by Becky's father, and the worlds within worlds they contain, which are also my worlds. Love-seat on which sixty years ago my parents were engaged to be married. A collection of heart-shaped stones gathered from northern lakeshores. Poster of a cat at ease, and the caption: *How beautiful it is to do nothing, and then to rest afterwards.* An empty seven-cent *7 Up* bottle of childhood, when pop used to back up through my nose. And now Duke Ellington's jazz coming on — this wizard who merely took the energy it takes to pout (he said) and wrote some blues.

And when the house and music fall silent, Becky's bells sound again, and I see that the clatter in my mind has gone still.

☾

Shortly before I turned thirteen, my family, which by now included two younger sisters, moved from our little white house in the village of Laird to an acreage at its south edge. All the buildings there were old. The house was an unpainted, misshapen structure that Dad went right to work renovating. For months we lived with sawdust and paint fumes, all this inside work being done after first taking care of our animals and working the farmland out in the country.

Our driveway was the last village street — named George Street — with the schoolyard on one side and our own cow pasture on the other. At the end, the road turned abruptly into the yard where the house stood just a few steps from the backstop of the ball diamond. Everyone at school saw our comings and goings. At recess I wanted badly to impress some girls, but always there were the odours of our beasts and the noise of rattletrap vehicles going by as Dad headed to the farm — beat-up Fargo half-ton, rusty International three-ton, and often with some decrepit implement in tow he'd bought and made serviceable. The boys at school nicknamed me Porkchops (or Porky for short), not because I was fat but because of the omnipresent pigs so close to the school.

On winter Mondays our kitchen was hung with stiff laundry on wooden racks obscuring what little light came through the one north window of the room, and for lunch (which we called dinner) my mother always cooked the boiled potatoes and sauerkraut I came to loathe with all my heart. Winter Saturdays were devoted to cleaning barns — chicken barn, cow barn, and pig barn, usually in that order so the chicken straw could form a bed on the stoneboat to contain the sloppier shit of pigs and cows. Even so, juices leaked from the sides as I hauled one load after another out to pasture with a Massey-Harris 30 tractor and its steel-cold seat to spread the shit around, where in spring it would thaw and add worse odours to the schoolyard air. Then I drove through Grandpa Gliege's garden to help clean his chicken barn, too, and fertilize his garden which was as close to the school on the west side as our pasture was on the south.

I was in my mid-teens by now. There were some escapes from farm work. Our garden was sheltered by a caragana hedge with a row of fruit trees on the inside, where I ate plums and crabapples as they ripened. The west end of the acreage bordered the Canadian National Railway tracks running north to Carlton where the trains turned around, and south to the city of Saskatoon forty miles distant. There beside the tracks under open skies I flew kites I had built from scavenged strips of wood and sheets of brown wrapping paper from Don's Groceteria. During summer holidays, if I had any spare time I'd sit against a sunny granary wall and write poems about chimney smoke rising straight up on bitter winter days. And on summer nights I'd sit in the verandah on the east side of the house, looking over the now-empty schoolyard, or a mile to the south where I could just make out Pat Hardy's farmhouse and a poplar bush I'd have loved to take her into.

Saskatoon's skyline back then was just the Robin Hood Flour mill and the smoking funnel of the Bessborough Hotel. In the heart of the city the CNR station seemed a royal palace where redcaps carried luggage and loudspeakers announced from a great dome the eastbound Supercontinental taking on passengers. Most of our family business was done in the Riversdale area, where Sam the Jewish merchant flipped bolts of cloth for my mother's sewing and sold Cracker Jack behind the counter (one box had a ballpoint pen for a prize and I felt as if I'd won a lottery), Cut-Rate Fruits where Grandma Gliege bought her beloved figs, and Empire Meats for Grandpa's rings of garlic sausage which we would eat on the long drive home. And Dominion Junk and Metal where Dad found a used furnace to install in the cellar of our house, a SAAN store for clothes, and the Chinese café where I always ordered veal cutlets and chocolate milk because they tasted so good after the sauerkraut of home and the pale blue milk that tasted of stinkweed our cows ate in the pasture.

Under the awning of Adilman's Department Store a deaf-mute vendor named "Popcorn Pete" always stood with his red cart, and inside the store a shoe lady looked disdainfully on country hicks like us as we tried on new shoes. And the basement — I couldn't imagine any toy department half as good as Adilman's, not even Eaton's on "the other side," as we called all of Saskatoon across the CN railyards. And later, in my teens, the men's washroom in the basement had a free stall with arousing graffiti, and another one which cost a nickel, which I paid only once and seeing it had no such titillation never wasted money on it again.

My family never owned a television set. It was considered sinful. I spent many adolescent evenings listening to religious broadcasts through a little plastic Gem radio on the kitchen shelf. I ordered their free literature, and at nights studied it under a bare forty-watt light bulb while wrapped in a brown army surplus sleeping bag in one corner of the cellar beside the cistern lid. I slept there by my own choice, because it was the most private spot in the house. I read *Christian Youth and Entertainment* and *Christian Youth and Dating*, this latter booklet borrowed from Jim and read furtively since it was so close to forbidden fruit.

The furnace Dad had bought stood hulking in the middle of the cellar floor, and beside it sat a cupboard where he "hid" a sex education book, not realizing I'd already found it earlier in one of his workshop drawers under a heap of bolts and rusty pipes. Most of what I wanted to know wasn't included in the book, and too much of what I didn't want was there. It warned about self-abuse, how my handshake would become feeble if I masturbated (though that word was never used) and I wouldn't be able to look other people in the eye. But much worse, I'd squander the life force of which God had granted me only a limited supply; if it was shot off prematurely there'd be none left for its proper use after I was married. Lying on my cot in the brown bag I'd repent of having abused myself, and read another chapter of *Christian Maturity*, which I hoped sometime to achieve, while hoping also to attend more Christian youth and entertainment functions in the near shit-shovelling future, and maybe even go on a real Christian date.

But the Russians were coming! At school the teachers warned that if (and more likely when) the bomb was dropped on Saskatoon, we'd see a flash in Laird and the eerie glow in the sky would give us only a few minutes to huddle under the cellar stairs, which was the safest place to be if the house collapsed in a blast of nuclear wind. But this was the spot where Dad had built a potato bin, and we'd have to hide there for weeks to escape the fallout, and if there wasn't enough of Mom's canning down there and we maybe had to go out to the barn for eggs we'd get something worse than leprosy that would turn our skins putrid, and for sure we'd die unless we stayed in the potato bin for God only knew how long.

One day in the post office I pulled a magazine from the mailbox titled *Our Northern Neighbors*. The cover showed a picture of Nikita Khrushchev and Fidel Castro hugging each other and waving for the camera. My name was printed on the bottom label, and this threw me into fresh panic. Who had sent this? How did they get my name? And if the bomb was about to scorch us, was I being warned to join the Communist party to stay safe — and wasn't that just what the religious booklets warned Russia would do before the Great Tribulation came, and if I wasn't a real Christian the Rapture would leave me behind on earth where I'd be forced to worship the Antichrist and endure the horrors of the Battle of Armageddon.

And at the end came the most terrifying thing of all — the Judgement of the Great White Throne. There I'd stand, blistered with radiation and bones full of Strontium-90 and hear God's verdict: *To hell with you, sinner.*

☾

Today ten thousand frozen crabapples are being transformed into five hundred waxwings — red and yellow, black and white and grey. I stand for twenty minutes watching them whir between an apple tree by the sidewalk and a great weeping birch across the way.

Wingbeats on eardrums, brushes at my winter coat.

☾

Ellen needed a break from the stress of attending to Brent, who's still in hospital recovering from his surgery. She invited me to go with her to Bud's on Broadway to hear some blues. Larraine was working late, and I was tired but agreed to go. The weather was unusually warm, and in early evening we walked a half hour to the bar, and when Jack Semple opened with a tight version of "Midnight Hour" I was already glad we'd gone.

Ellen was in dancing mode, and knowing my Mennonite reticence she left me with my thoughts at the table while she pulled others to the floor. I watched them, though, recalling William Blake's lines, *Dear Mother, dear Mother, the Church is cold, but the Ale-house is healthy & pleasant & warm.*

Long after midnight we ambled back home. The air was still warm, ice crystals diffused the light of the street lamps, and it was a magic street we walked. Ellen was wasted, I was Johnny Two-Moons myself, and we gabbed so hard we feared being arrested on drunk and disorderly charges. We wondered at this rare friendship, being able to enjoy a night like this without romantic or sexual conundrums, or worries that our partners might be offended. Ellen as usual tormented me with my country origins, "Above all, Lloyd, you'll always be a pig farmer."

I got her in the door and let her climb her own stairs, and went to sit on the riverbank. When I finally went to bed around 2:30, I slept (I nearly said) the sleep of the just.

How the blues makes an art of ego's grumbles.

((

One winter afternoon when I was fourteen I stood behind my house with a forty-gallon drum and a water hose, flooding a patch in the garden to make a skating rink. But I felt joyless and guilty as I waited for the barrel to fill, dumped it and waited for a refill, and finally I made a vow: "This is the day I'm fixing up the mess."

For much of the previous year I had shoplifted from all three of the stores in the village — the Co-op, the Variety Shop, and Don's Groceteria. Often I'd come out with pockets stuffed full of chocolate bars and chewing gum, and especially cigarettes which I gave away at school to those whose friendship I craved. So notorious had my reputation grown that some had even taken to placing orders. One day Big Steve in his leather jacket and duck's-ass haircut raised his shades and said, "Ratzlaff, I smoke Matinee King-size Filters — anything else you can keep." And sometimes it seemed the guys did like me, but not even these hoods were willing to rob our stores blind, with threats of reform school so regularly in the air.

Late that winter afternoon when my parents came home, I drained the hose and followed them into the house, and in the kitchen spilled my confession.

There was a dumb silence. When my father recovered, he pulled three chairs from the table and set them in a half-circle. We knelt down with our elbows on the seats, and my parents began praying for this wayward son who had just gone from bad to very worst.

When we got to our feet, Dad went straight to the telephone and made three calls, and within the hour we were headed to town in the old '46 Chevrolet Stylemaster, where I would confess to the merchants I'd defrauded and repay them with money borrowed from my parents, of which they had precious little.

We parked at one end of Main Street in front of the Co-op. Dad went inside to fetch the manager while I waited in the back seat. Bruno Neufeld came out and sat beside me, and my parents listened in as I admitted what I'd done, and the manager only said, "Well, that's not very nice." Dad took out his wallet and paid the bill, which I had already estimated as closely as possible.

In the middle of the block stood the Variety Shop, which other than the hotel was the most sinful place in town with a pinball machine, pool tables, and a Wurlitzer jukebox I never got a chance to play. Mr. Kleist came out and listened silently as I repeated the account of my wrongdoing, and with no word of thanks or of condemnation accepted the money and returned to his work.

But at the far end of the street stood Don's Groceteria, where our family did most of its business, which had taken by far the greatest hit. Don Regier climbed into the back seat of the car as the other two had, and listened to a third account of my transgressions, my words more repentant than ever. Dad sat behind the steering wheel and Mom interjected, "It's awful! We knew other kids did such things, but never thought our son would turn out like this."

The storekeeper laid a hand on my shoulder, and said, "I knew about it. Your Grandpa's neighbour told me long ago, but I decided not to mention it to your parents because I knew one day you'd come to make it right." Then he told a story of a boy carrying a bag of feathers in a strong wind, how the bag blew open and the feathers scattered and he could never get them back again. I supposed the moral was that whatever's been done can't be undone, yet the merchant's tone of voice and hand on my shoulder let me think that maybe my sins weren't as unpardonable as they seemed.

We came to the matter of restitution. He spread the fingers of one hand and held them up and said, "Suppose we settle for five packs of cigarettes?" But this I could not accept, knowing that the real number must have been far closer to fifty.

I only know that when we got home late that night, after a very silent supper I went to bed with both a clear conscience and a bill totalling over a hundred dollars — a monstrous debt I'd have to work off through a long year to come.

After that I never stole another thing. If ever I got too cocky for my dad's liking he'd only say, "Look out, boy, maybe you've forgotten you still owe me money."

One day thirty years after those juvenile crimes, I attended my hometown's seventy-fifth anniversary celebration. I went back to Don's store — now renamed a Shop-Rite — to thank the gentle merchant for having once incarnated such a rare grace in my impoverished world. The other two stores had long gone out of business, but Mr. Regier was behind his counter as always. He listened as I recalled my youthful follies and replied that lately he had been struggling with a sense of futility. "For forty years I've sold groceries in this town," he said, "but what have I done that amounted to anything?"

I turned to leave and he took my hand, adding that the visit had helped him think perhaps he'd done something after all.

((

Jim is prone to dismiss his dreams in the common way of our culture, but when I went to pick him up for a drive he could hardly wait to tell me what he called "the most powerful experience of my life." He insisted he was *not* asleep when it happened, but groped for an appropriate label: "It was a dream with clearly defined boundaries, or something like that."

It was at 1:40 AM — he was precise — that a colleague from the Physics Department who'd died a year ago stood by his bedside wearing the familiar blue lab coat and a grin that in their coffee room had usually signalled the beginnings of a political harangue. This time he said only, "Jim!" but when Jim reached to touch him, he vanished.

I asked what he thought the experience could mean, and he said, "Nothing," but re-emphasized that it had not been a mere dream, and he had not been asleep when it happened.

☾

Last night I could hardly sit through the second act of *West Side Story* at Larraine's school. A few hours earlier a bitch of a toothache had taken hold, and afterwards when I went to bed full of pain medication, I found it didn't work and lying down only made the pain worse. Larraine had to sleep in another room, and for most of the night I sat up in bed or knelt like a penitent at the open window drawing frigid air through my teeth — which momentarily eased the pain before the next wave hit.

I pounded the pillow, nearly wept, never slept at all. This was a demon not to be cast out.

Today the dentist said the tooth is not cracked, but it may have formed a calcium deposit. While writing out a prescription he said, "It's like an oyster forms a pearl," and I moaned, "Too bad it's not worth money."

How can a soul be so tyrannized by a tooth? I begin to think I know who I am, then a molar catches fire and blows my identity and so-called spirituality all to hell.

Benjamin Franklin's infallible remedy for toothache: "Soak the root of the aching tooth in vinegar, and set it in the sun to dry for half an hour."

☾

Downtown two identical houses were being demolished to make room for another high-rise. Cement walks still led up to the stoops and screened porches, storm shutters on bay windows were held in place by wing nuts, and the second-storey dormers stood erect above the street. The houses looked as fine as any sung by Crosby, Stills, Nash & Young — I could almost see the two cats in the yards.

But one house was only half there. A machine named Deere was reaching, clawing, crunching at the roof and gables. At each assault the naked west wall swayed, showed off the green paint of an upstairs bedroom and the wood shavings of its insulation, the chimney shivered and then stood motionless again above the open fireplace.

The Deere's operator, I thought, could hardly be called a driver. His machine turned in a bare half-circle — chomp *beepbeep*, crunch *beepbeep*, forever.

I was on my way to a meeting, but began scribbling a few thoughts until a semi pulled up behind me and blared a horn — *Move along, Sonny, make way for demolition.*

In the late afternoon I drove home and stopped again at the site. The brontosaurus was scooping the last of the debris from the basement hole, a semi-trailer parked beside it overloaded with the building's remains.

The twin house stood in the fading light, its dormers about to close their eyes for the last time, perhaps to dream of dairy horses that once clopped by on the avenue below.

☾

Spring

Godfingering

I walked on a spring afternoon at the edge of the city. The winter had been long, and immense banks of snow were still thawing and running down to the river, which remained frozen on its far side and on the near shoreline was jumbled with heaps of ice. But the sun was warm, and I removed my jacket and tied the sleeves about my waist, and at a familiar spot turned onto a path running above the river.

A small boat drifted in mid-stream. She drew me along the slope to the verge of the bank, where it fell off steeply and the brush grew thick below. The vessel, unhurrying, turned her prow, and a fulgent light gleamed from her, as if she carried a great ingot of snow that had unmoored her, perhaps, when it broke from the bank, and she transported it now downriver.

Gradually she came on toward the willow saplings that hung over the water below my lookout, then shifted again, and I saw it was not snow that had dazzled my eye but sunbeams reflecting from the craft's metal hull. And now I made out an ensign and saw a ruby stripe shining on her side in the mid-afternoon light.

The boat nudged the shoreline, then backed off again, as if wilfully, turned slowly alongside the strand, nestled underneath the willows, and lay still.

Not far off there was a trail leading down through the tangle. I could go to her — then would I (but I dismissed the thought as it came) become a skiff owner by thievery? Or should I be a good neighbour at least, tether her to a branch, and go up and cry through the town — *LOST BOAT FOUND!* — put someone else's mind anyway to rest? Yet if a boat so took her own way, could anyone be said to possess her at all?

I began recalling childhood nights in my little white house, the bed under the slope of the rafters where I imagined it as a boat drifting into friendly darkness, into dreams that carried me away. And could this craft, all empty, want me to lie down within her to see where the river might take us?

Below me, the boat moved gently at the stern. As I lingered, she turned her prow toward the current, began floating again into a channel between the ice shards on this side of the river and the frozen expanse beyond, then drove into a northeasterly breeze that ruffled the surface where she went.

I followed on the upper path while she sailed below, and so we travelled side by side until she came to open water. There she turned her ruby stripe once more to the sun, blinding me for an instant, and swung back to follow a bend in the river just where my own trail turned up toward home.

How easy she lay on the water.

How simple the water was with her.

((

Brent has recovered enough to be brought home today in a Medi-van. Since our building has no elevator, Ellen had asked a few friends to be available to help carry him up to their third-floor apartment.

We wrestled the wheelchair up six flights of stairs, and near the top landing Brent's face tightened and went white, and as we parked him in his living room his eyes turned up slowly beneath their lids and he passed out. For an instant I was terrified — I saw Pluto in the third grade again — but then Brent was back, and we all cheered his return.

I asked him later where he'd "gone," and he said wistfully, "To a very peaceful place. It was like a kid jumping into a pile of leaves and snuggling down. I sort of hated to come back."

☾

Jim claims to have hope, yet today he repeated several times that there's nothing left for him here.

I had given him a recording of Garrison Keillor and the Hopeful Gospel Quartet in a Carnegie Hall concert, thinking that Keillor's reminiscences of some pleasant things in the old-time religion along with his good humour toward the bad might be a perfect gift for Jim.

He had listened to the album, but was perplexed that it was neither evangelism nor secular comedy, and he seemed troubled by whether or not Garrison was making fun of Christianity.

At one point in the discussion he said, "Anyone with a smattering of education knows it's meaningless to think of heaven as 'up there'." I asked him to say more about how he understood heaven, and his responses were all along the lines of "We were always told that . . . "

I'd say, "But I'd like to know how you imagine it, to help me understand what you're experiencing." This yielded only circular responses: golden streets might be figurative, the heavenly throne may be symbolic, but the God sitting on the throne is real.

☾

I didn't sow my wild oats, then complete an education, find a job, marry, and procreate. I did things more or less backwards.

After high school I attended a southern Saskatchewan Bible institute for two years, a place which many of my relatives had recommended. Jim himself had met Laura, his wife there, and in my second year I met a woman who had just arrived for her first. I saw her one evening in the supper lineup along the opposite wall of Dickson Dining Hall, attractive but somewhat aloof, I thought, and learned that she came from Dauphin, Manitoba. Even the name of her town sounded exotic, and a day later when we were introduced I also discovered that she had a brother named Graham — a back name for a front name, as some Mennonites said — which she pronounced *Grayum*, not *Gray-Ham* as my people did the famous evangelist Billy's surname.

Immediately she was forbidden fruit. Not only for being non-Mennonite, which to me was mysterious enough, but because this school existed to train people for God's work, which implied among other things that romantic involvements among students were forbidden. The principal in his revival campaigns to my parents' generation had already "saved" half of Salem Church, the congregation from which Jim and I had sprung. My extended family revered this man, who liked to point out that his institute granted *diplomas*, not degrees like certain uppity colleges did in their compromises with the wicked world. In his school, students were forbidden to date or even to communicate with the opposite sex unless for "Christian" reasons.

We saw how those who broke his rules were handled. One shy young Pennsylvania Dutchman so uncouth that he ate his eggs shell-and-all had the misfortune of falling in love with a

Mennonite girl from British Columbia, and went so far as to visit her during Christmas vacation. When classes resumed in January he faced the principal, who'd already heard about it, and on threat of expulsion stood at the front of the chapel weeping openly as he confessed his sin, already considered half unfit for God's service. (The girl was spared, however, in a curious reversal of the biblical story of the woman dragged up to Jesus for stoning — "caught in the very act of adultery," her accusers said, with no mention of any man involved.)

In the chapel audience that day sat a skulking mouse of a faculty member who in his own student years had been chastised by the principal for falling in love with a fellow student. But he had made amends, and married the woman, and returned to the institute to teach Bible and music classes. Often he played his accordion and trumpet in chapel, both instruments at once, his left hand working the keyboard and the right fingering God's own horn.

Another teacher was Ukrainian but liked to pretend he was Scottish. He wore tartans and rolled his *r*'s while delivering lectures and sermons, every one with an alliterated seven-point outline. In my first year I had joined the school choir, and this man had accompanied us on a summer tour. We were billeted in private homes, and some of us had watched him hanging girls' underwear on the hosts' backyard wash lines as he did the laundry, and we felt both jealous of him and guilty for our lusts.

Now in my second year I was smitten with this woman from Dauphin. Eventually I wrote her a note on embossed stationery and sealed it in a matching blue envelope, and one night after prayer meeting gave it to a classmate to deliver to his own illicit girlfriend, who'd pass it on to the girl I hoped would become mine.

Her reply came back just as furtively, suggesting that perhaps it was God's will for us to be better acquainted. So our passion grew as the year went on, and we began making plans to move to Saskatoon in the spring, where she would live with an older sister who had moved there earlier, I'd find my own accommodations, and both of us would hunt for jobs.

On the final day of school, after the graduation ceremony, we left in my car for Saskatoon. Long after midnight, on the road somewhere near Rosetown, I was so exhausted that for an instant I "saw" a giant spider in the middle of the highway, but didn't mention it because my girlfriend had laid a hand on my knee, and the last thing I wanted was for her to remove it. We arrived in the city just as the sun was coming up, stopped at a park two blocks from her sister's apartment, and lay down under a tree, free at last, thank God Almighty, to be together.

She found a secretarial job with the National Farmers Union, I was hired as an accounting clerk for Massey Ferguson Limited, and that fall we had a shotgun marriage. Not because of pregnancy — there had been no sex, but the wedding was no less urgent for that.

For our disobedience the principal banned us from returning to his institute. Although the campus did have a married students' residence, it was not for couples like us, he wrote, "who had formed attachments arising right in Bible school life."

A great many of my own relatives were pastors and missionaries, and it had hardly occurred to me that I would not follow in their steps. Any other jobs were a mere preamble to the true vocation, and within a year of marriage I had applied to a college in Winnipeg and been accepted.

As that autumn approached, we both resigned from our jobs. The day came when we packed our possessions into a 1963 Chevrolet Bel Air, its trunk loaded to the hinges with stereo equipment Jim had built and sold to us. We strapped other boxes and suitcases to the roof rack and bundled them in a woollen blanket, which only a few miles out of Saskatoon began flapping in the wind as its ends came undone.

I was headed for college, one step up from an institute, and would get a degree after all.

(

Today my mother phoned with some news. Her sister, Jim's mother, "has the same trouble as Royal Schmidt — it's a problem at the top of the head."

I inquired what sort of problem it might be, and she explained, "It's kind of a bad feeling, similar to dizziness and yet not dizziness."

As for the fickle spring weather we're having on the prairies, she said, "It shall snow yet this night," and added, "Otherwise, news there are none."

(

Larraine and Ellen went out for the evening, and I sat with Brent from five until midnight. We made soup and Montreal smoked meat sandwiches. I helped with his toileting and exercises and gave him back massages. We played Canadian Trivia and he beat me by a nose.

He told me of a vision he'd seen the night before, and insisted — as Jim had done — that he was awake at the time. He'd just rubbed his eyes, and when he opened them a dazzling white cross stood at the foot of his bed, and remained there for about twenty seconds before fading away. His first comment after reporting this was that he didn't know what it meant.

I asked what the crucifix on his wall meant.

☾

The Evangelical Mennonite Brethren church in which Jim and I were raised had a small congregation in Winnipeg of about forty members and as many "adherents" — people who attended regularly but had not seen fit to join. While I was completing my degree in religious studies, this group invited me to become their minister after I graduated.

The denominational headquarters in Omaha, Nebraska granted me a temporary license to conduct pastoral duties, but only after rebuking me (benignly enough) for not adhering quite strictly to their brand of theology, which I didn't then realize had already displaced a more authentic Anabaptist heritage at least a generation before I was born.

All Mennonite churches practice congregational rather than episcopal governance, and pastors are hired by majority vote of local members, with no hierarchy of bishops to overrule. Thus, with enough neuroses to last a lifetime and a stiff dose of original sin to boot, I began defending God's ways to God's people, my head full of the King James Bible and sermons spiced with Hebrew and Greek etymologies for added effect.

In two years at this church there was one wedding, one baptism, two communion services, and no funerals at all. The workload nevertheless was formidable — sermons every Sunday morning and night (some evenings with only five or six people present), Wednesday night study and prayer sessions, Friday night youth groups, hospital and home visits, and the expected "outreach" to the larger St. Vital community to attract more people to church. For this work my wife and I were given a pittance, from which we had to pay utilities on the drafty parsonage beside the church, which in the coldest winter months burned up nearly a third of our income in heating bills alone.

When our first daughter Shannon was born, I also began working at unskilled labour jobs to help make ends meet. This I was required to give up when a board member who had privately told me "I love you like my own son" got to hear about it. Then he confronted me publicly: "We pay you to work in *church*, not someplace else."

After the first year, I informed the board that we could no longer afford to license our car and would have to park it indefinitely. The chairman, one of the wealthiest members with a thriving business and a private airplane said, "Good for you, Lloyd — I wish I could do without my car." Other members drove fancy vehicles and owned revenue houses, but not one person suggested giving us a raise. That night after the meeting I walked along Avalon Road in the dark choking back angry tears, and thought I understood why this church in the fourteen years of its existence had already had seven ministers.

It may have been the next day that I decided to register for part-time university classes. I was afraid to do this, having been taught that the world is hellbound and we chosen people were few, but already I wanted the "more" that a secular education seemed to promise. I wasn't yet prepared for the liberal arts, but enrolled in a psychology program at the University of Winnipeg, hoping against my fear to become also a little less of a conundrum to myself.

After the second year, we received an invitation from a larger congregation in Morris, known as Manitoba's "Stampede Town" south of Winnipeg, to a half-time position which along with extra janitorial duties paid a higher salary than the city church had done full-time. So our small family moved, at first into a cramped and mouse-ridden basement suite which the new board chairman called "cozy." The Omaha council renewed my license, and for the next few years I commuted to Winnipeg twice a week for classes. I began reading with a fervour bordering on greed, and more widely than ever before. I joined an ecumenical organization whose aims were to apply psychology to religious life. At the university I reluctantly began opening to friendships with professors and students — some of them with women, never sexual but still with an emotional turbulence that felt liberating in ways I could not have imagined before.

My wife did not share these new enthusiasms. The marriage soon began to be sad, though not yet broken, and it was a bitter-sweet day when we welcomed our new daughter Sheri into the world.

By now the Omaha elders had granted three temporary licenses, and began requesting me to be ordained. They had no power to require this, and none to dismiss me if I refused, as long as my congregation wished me to stay. But I was in my early thirties now, chafing at fundamentalism's yoke and unwilling to be ordained, at any rate by this denomination. I applied to several universities for graduate studies in counselling psychology, and was accepted — miraculously it seemed — at the University of Saskatchewan, with a generous scholarship besides.

When I resigned from the church, it was almost exactly seven years since we had left Saskatoon. Now we returned with our five- and three-year-old daughters, and I at least began to feel free from the clutches of a godawful religion.

I was not a very good shepherd, but at least I ran from the sheep before I devoured them.

☾

When Shannon was small, I saw her one morning struggling to put on a shirt that had got reversed in the laundry. She noticed me watching and explained, "I have to uninside-out this thing."

Sometimes she saw me heading for the door and asked, "Where are you going?"

"I'm going to work," I'd say — or wherever it was.

Sometimes she thought I was leaving when I was only going down to the basement or out to the yard, and I'd say, "No, I'm not going anywhere."

Then there were times I really was leaving, and she'd ask, "Are you going nowhere?"

One day shortly after her sister was born, she came to visit me at the church office with a bag of cookies she and her mother had baked. I watched from a foyer window as she came dawdling up the street, stopping here and there to pick flowers from people's yards, and arriving at the church door with the cookies in one hand and a half-wilted bouquet in the other.

We had a little tea party in church that afternoon, she and I, and when she left for home I watched again through the window until she rounded a corner, and went back to my half-written sermon. Instead I found myself composing a sentimental poem about all things fading like flowers in my baby's fist, half-aware that I was at the edge of a religious world her mother and I had grown up in, and that I was destined to get off.

((

Spring equinox, and the seventh anniversary of my father's death. These days the sun rises straight east and sets straight west, dirty water runs down to the drains, and the river takes what it gets.

Trees are greening under blue skies, red-winged blackbirds lilt on a wire, a gopher barely up from underground lies squashed to the pavement, tail waving like a little stripe in the wind.

Across the street, in Diefenbaker Park, the ground is littered with branches from a windstorm last fall. They've lain through the winter holding enough life to sprout new shoots, and unless park attendants cart them away, the new saplings will have rooted before another winter comes.

An unseen bird cavorts in a bush. When I listen to it my headache vanishes. If I give up on the bird, my aching head returns.

((

As a graduate student with a head and body full of steam, I began often to dream about trains. Many times in these dreams I clung terrified to a huge headlamp as a locomotive hurtled toward Carlton at the end of the CNR line of my youth. In another dream my parents ordered me to "go and drive some engines," but at the rail yards I was afraid I couldn't do it, and thought I'd have to return home and tell them. Or again, I'd be seated between two women engineers taking their train only they knew where.

On a sidetrack between the stockyards and railway station of my hometown, I'm perched on the ledge of an old steam locomotive where the engineer and I are having an amicable chat. Suddenly a diesel train rushes by on the parallel track, coming within inches of hitting us. The passengers shout derogatory remarks at us about being slow and old-fashioned. Their train pulls sharply to a stop at the station, and in a flash leaves again for Carlton. I begin to sob, knowing that the new train is destined to replace the one we're on.

☾

Although graduate studies held more than enough academic tedium, the program came fairly easily to me, and within two years my course work and thesis were complete. Shortly afterwards I was hired in a temporary position at the University of Saskatchewan counselling centre, where I had previously worked in completing my internship.

One day a young woman came for help. She was in her final term of an honours psychology program, and within minutes I'd learned that her grades were consistently high, her professors had long favoured her for graduate work of her own, promising scholarships and joint research projects and publications listing her as junior author.

Then she set me a task: "I've decided to quit, but I want you to talk me out of it."

Without doubt this was the most unusual problem I'd encountered to that point in my career. Her terms were clear enough, and for several weeks I did try to meet them. Every few days she came in and I mustered additional reasons for her to continue: only two months until convocation — why not finish the degree? You can always decline scholarships later, but why burn your bridges now? Think how proud your parents will be when seeing you graduate *summa cum laude.*

Every suggestion was met with a "yes, but," and try as I would to follow her original injunction she refused to be dissuaded, and one day I said, "I've done everything I can. If you want to quit, quit."

She drew a deep breath and smiled, but when she left I had no idea how I could possibly have been of any use.

In my own studies I had read the psychologist Carl Rogers who told of a client who came to him in a quandary which, after many sessions, had not been resolved. In what proved to be their final meeting, the young man said, "I don't know *what* I'm going to do — but *I'm* going to do it." At that moment, Rogers said, he knew he could safely leave this man to his own devices, though with characteristic humility he observed that nonetheless it had taken another person's presence and attention for the insight to be reached.

One day a month later when most of the staff was gone and I was on duty alone, the young student visited again without having made an appointment. She came hobbling through the door on a pair of crutches, but with a face more radiant than I'd ever seen it. She sank into her usual chair, propped the crutches in a corner, and said, "Well, I did quit."

I didn't know whether to congratulate her. She began recounting how she'd endured her professors' wrath, her parents' chagrin, the perplexity of nearly all her friends. The degree had been left unfinished, the scholarships unclaimed, and instead she'd gone on a ski holiday and broken her leg.

As she ended the story, she picked up her crutches and with another chuckle said, "You know, this is the first time in my life I've ever done anything I really wanted."

((

My father suffered his first heart attack at the age of sixty-five, and after that he began to age visibly. By then I had come at least some way past my delayed adolescent rebellion, and occasionally began asking him to tell me some stories from his youth. He almost always demurred, claiming that he had nothing of interest to say.

But sometimes I'd overhear him tell a story to a few of his friends, and began asking him instead to write down some memories. He usually protested at this, too — there wasn't much to say, and besides, his spelling was so poor.

One day as I tried again to coax out one of his reluctant anecdotes, I hinted that by staying on the family farm he must have been closer to his father than his siblings were. This only drew a scoff — "*Nobody* was close to him." Then I remembered my mother saying that on their wedding day the old man had told his son, *Met die jeft et nuscht* — with you it gives nothing.

Once when Dad knew he was to be hospitalized for a week on a matter unrelated to his ailing heart, he took an orange Hilroy scribbler with him, and while convalescing filled up six pages with a dense and laborious script that crowded at the margins. They are lines I treasure.

> We had neighbours about a half mile from our place, and when we went to school we usually went by their Place and they walked with us to school. This was a Peters family. Mr. Peters wife had died, and another

family by the name of Peters where the Husband had been attacked by a pig. and bitten Him died, then these two spouse, got to hear of each other and got married. They each had a family so it happened that they each had a (peter.) so we called one Big Peter and the other one little Peter.

Little Peter usually had to cut wood into stove length so he would ask one of us to hold the stick or small tree, then He would chop into it with the axe on the chopping Block. and then he would give a blow on the cut end to break it off. and it would Jar our hands and arms, it realy hurt us. , then we would say we did not want to hold the sticks any more. He would promise us he would not do it again but usually after a few pieces he would do it again. But anyway they were good friends of ours.

My Dad had some sheep at the time and they were fenced in on our yard so they were always around. There was a buck with them. and he was an ornary one. mean as could be. He usually would sneak up behind you give you a good bump. One day he was after me, and I ran as fast as I could but he got me anyway and pushed me right into that slough were the Pistol was thrown into I was just plastered with mud.

My Uncle Jake lived about ¾ of a mile from us and one day He was caring water from the well to the house, and the old buck thought this was a good time for him to have some fun. so He'd come and bump him from the back, He just could not get away from Him, so He'd grab him Throw him down and roll him onto his Back with all four legs in the air, then hed take his Pail of water and run as fast as he could this way he was able to get quite a ways towards the house till hed have to repeat the Process.

Then one day Big Peter was at our Place and we got the brain wave of playing a trick on that old buck. If we would stand in the door way of the barn and tease him, he would come charging us. Then Big Peter would hold onto the top of the door frame and lift himself up. and Buck would not hit anything. They charge with their eyes closed when they are about to hit you, so he could not figure out why he did not hit anything. and soon quit. Then we thought of another Idea. We held up a big flat stone and let him come and bash into it. He did not do this to many times either He shake His head and go away.

After writing these few pages in his hospital bed, my father lived on for another half-dozen years but he never touched the scribbler again.

((

The gulls of Wanuskewin cry urgently overhead while a meadowlark sings from a fence post. In the distance, I hear Black Elk's "thunder beings" approach.

Mosquitoes cannot bite the bronze bull, his cock as low to the ground as his beard.

One thunder questions, another rolls a reply. The sculpted woman knows them by name, and the name of the cloud peering low over her tepee.

A spatter of raindrops, a scent of honey on the southern breeze.

Something flutters — what shall I name it?

☾

Our granddaughter Katy in Kelowna is about to turn two. She's already memorized many children's books and likes to "read" them aloud to others, though she's just beginning to sound out words for herself. She has only the concept *tomorrow* for anything in the future. One day on the telephone I asked whether she'd come to visit us sometime in Saskatoon and she said firmly, "No! You will come to visit here tomorrow, and at autumn, and at Christmas."

It's not that time seems endless to her, but that she has no notion of time, nothing at all like the old hymn from my youth, *The trumpet of the Lord shall sound and time shall be no more.* For her there is only an endless compendium of "somewhats" — shimming (swimming), shinging (swinging), candies, flowers, kitties, and ants that taste just like strawberries.

She will grow up, as her mother did, and time will come into being. By adolescence she'll have become theoretically finite to herself, and by adulthood will know finitude as direct experience. Then in her maturity perhaps she'll be reborn to see heaven in a wildflower and live in eternity's sunrise — something she does now without thinking about it.

This morning Shannon called to say that for the first time Katy had brought *her* some flowers. I said I hoped she'd write a better poem about it than I did for her. And late in the evening, here I am staring at photos of two little squirts grinning at me from the bookshelf, one dear daughter, and her daughter equally grand and dear.

((

Until now Jim has remembered very few of his dreams, but today he seemed eager to repeat one that's come to him four or five times since our last visit.

He's in a vacant house. A heap of yellow and purple glass shards lies in the middle of the living room floor. He reaches to touch it, and bright-coloured Lucite cubes spring out and roll into the far corners of the room, leaving behind a small skin ("sort of like a lobster skin") that had held them together.

Now he wanders through the rest of the house, but returns again to the cubes in the living room. He doesn't do anything with them, just lets them lie.

I asked what these cubes brought to his mind. He pondered a while and said, "Maybe they're about play." Privately I was afraid of the broken shards, the empty house, and the dead skin, but I urged him to play with those cubes if he ever finds himself in that house again.

((

Often it seems I've made no progress in taming the mind, and formal meditation only makes it more obstreperous. I had hoped for an orderly progression from the first faltering visions to a full and permanent enlightenment — another ungranted wish — and instead have to return to step one, not merely once a day but countless times per hour.

Yet there's no way to unlearn the necessity of this. Is the mind messy? Start again to clear it — what else?

When I met the woman who married me, I thought she could redress some of my subculture's wrongdoings, and discovered she had endured abuses of her own which it seemed I might help to remedy, so that together we'd have a belated renaissance, together become the good husband and wife we resolved to be. It was a pathetic union — a wife expected to be also stepmother and muse, a husband turning into a father and pastor before having properly reached his own adolescence. When I began studying psychology, one professor said to me privately with all the kindness that had so endeared him in class, "Lloyd, you're doing in your mid twenties what most people do at fourteen."

The religion in which Jim and I were raised had taught us to abjure the clerical and sacramental theologies of mainline Christendom, which we accused of having only the outer shell of faith and not its inner reality. Our great watchword was "saved by grace alone," yet it was a rare experience to feel grace actually taking hold of us. In my first year as a minister I bought a set of New Testament commentaries by William Barclay, an Anglican scholar, who noted that the Greek word for grace — *charis* — meant something like "charm." At first I suspected this of being a piece of sophistry (the old substitutionary atonement theology was anything but charming); then as new people appeared in my life to incarnate the missing charm, I came to find Barclay's notion very appealing indeed, and the old blood sacrifice theology began to seem preposterous, if not yet quite unthinkable.

In the early years of marriage I imagined that many wrongs were being righted and deficits compensated, thereby proving the biblical aphorism, *When I am weak, then I am strong.* I believed that I understood paradox and metaphor, how opposite things can be equally true, and how identities may overlap. Such breakdowns of logic became familiar experiences, though I was humiliated anew at each reminder that this is no lesson to be learned once for all, but which reimposes itself at any level of understanding I suppose I've reached. Hadn't the gospels warned that the first shall be last, the rich poor, those who cling to life will lose it but let it go and it's found? One biblical commentator went so far as to say that certain promises are best honoured by repenting of having made them.

Then how could I be orthodox, when all was paradox?

Newfound strengths turned into weaknesses, as if there were some Deity after all out to prove the converse of St. Paul's aphorism: *When you think you are strong, you're weaker than you could guess.* Eventually, on the far side of a prolonged and bitter divorce, it seemed unsafe to suppose I understood anything at all. On the Day of Judgment the bewildered sheep on the right hand ask, *When did we visit you, feed you, comfort you?* while the goats on the left, equally bewildered, bleat, *When didn't we clothe you, when didn't we cast out devils in your name?*

It was a combined blow and illumination when I first *saw* the text in St. John (though I'd read it often before): "If you were blind, you would not be guilty; but because you say, 'We see,' therefore your guilt remains."

When did I do this, when didn't I do that?

((

For nearly three months Brent has contended with recurring knee infections. Now he's been hospitalized again, and his fractured leg will have to be reopened. This long regress/progress/regress is defying his notions of hope, which have tended to mean "getting back to the way things were." He's been bedridden or hitching along on crutches for so many weeks that his optimism has taken a thrashing, his wings clipped with no foreseeable flights in the future.

Today he talked about his depression. When I reminded him of the countless ways he'd helped me through my own dark times in the long division and aftermath of divorce, he wept — something he rarely does — and gave me a hug.

☾

Jim's older son Jeff says the doctors have given the family a blunt forecast. First, "the human things will fade." Then his body will begin shutting down; and by the end he'll have curled up like a foetus, and will die. Apparently the physicians sounded confident about what "the human things" are, and that their diction itself had been humane.

Bindy hasn't yet been informed.

Today when Laura led him into the living room he looked like a ghost. She settled him on the couch and I asked where his mind goes these days. Mostly nowhere, he said. He sleeps and sleeps, and when he's awake tries to read but finds his attention span very short.

A colleague from the physics department had given him a book on spirituality, which he said "didn't even refer to Scripture," as if this were an anomaly. His own leather-bound King James Bible lay beside him on an end table. I had wondered often whether he might like me to read something from it, and today when I offered he said yes.

I chose the 139th psalm, and the words that struck him most were, "If I ascend up into heaven, thou art there: if I make my bed in hell, behold, thou art there." I very much wished to know how he understood this, but he wasn't inclined to ponder it for himself, and said, "I should get my commentary and see what they say about that" ("they" being the evangelical theologians he'd read in his own Bible school days). He was too weak to get up and go looking for it, so I embarked (stupidly, it turned out) on a discussion of how things exist in our minds. He said he knew what I meant, "because if it's not in your mind, you don't experience it." Yet he couldn't sustain the thought, and quickly added, "If you go to Cuba, you have to get in an airplane and leave your mind behind."

I noted that the Cuba to which we fly is ultimately another mental image, perhaps different from any we've had before — but this was plainly unhelpful, and it became pointless to talk about God as being another mental image. So I quoted St. Paul in the New Testament addressing the Athenians on Mars Hill, *In God we live and move and have our being* — no way beyond deity, neither by ascending to heaven (as our psalmist said) nor by descending to hell, nor by navigating to earth's remotest ends.

This was still less helpful, and Jim said, "I'm keeping all my options about theology open. Maybe that's a chickenshit way of hanging on, but I don't want to burn any bridges."

Christ, I hated leaving him looking so defeated and feeling that way myself.

)

Coming out of the supermarket I realized I'd forgotten where I had parked my car, and for a while dithered about hoping no one would notice.

Finally I remembered in which stall I had left it, and realized I hadn't actually forgotten, only forgotten that I remembered.

☾

Easter Sunday. Larraine's taken her mother to mass at St. Augustine Church, and I've put on an old gospel album to wash some leftover party dishes by, along with ashtrays nearly as full as last night's moon. Andrae Crouch warms up to a Carnegie Hall crowd, *Hey! I want evvubuddy git tugethuh — this ain't a concert, we havin' SUH-viss!*

Every visit with Jim makes it more urgent for me to give up smoking. In an early attempt some years ago I went out one night for dinner at a favourite Chinese restaurant. The proprietor took my order and asked whether I'd like something from the bar. I declined, saying then I'd probably also have a smoke and I was trying hard to quit. He stood beside his bamboo curtain with a look somewhere between pity and amusement, and said, "Ah, all or nothing — that's the Western way. But the Chinese way" (here he added great emphasis) "*is knowing how to use.*"

Andraé Crouch rips into another tune, *Cain't nobody do me like Jesus, cain't nobody do me like the Lawd.* Jim and I grew up in a culture that considered smoking more sinful than harmful. Our Grandpa Gliege as a young man had battled the *Tabak* demon in converting from European Lutheranism to a small Mennonite sect that had migrated from the Crimea to settle in the state of South Dakota. Once, in a fit of repentance, he'd thrown his tobacco pouch far out in a stubble field, but next morning went looking for it again — and found it, too. Then standing there in the field he reasoned with himself, *Der Tabak ist staerker als ich* — this tobacco is stronger than I am. And by the grace of God he had cast it even farther afield, and in all the rest of his life never rolled another *Zigaret*.

His four sons all took up smoking. The two older ones continued for most of their lives, but the younger ones were eventually saved from it as Grandpa had been. One of them later bought a store in a small Alberta town, at first vowing to give up the previous merchant's policy of selling tobacco. Yet the demand was great, and the next year when our family went to visit, the cigarettes were still there behind the counter. Sometimes my uncle let me play storekeeper, and I felt most sophisticated when a customer asked for smokes.

"Give me a pack of Black Cat Cork-tips."

"Yes sir, there you go," *Ching-ching*.

On our fathers' side of the family, a younger uncle once flicked a live butt into a wheat field as he passed by in his buggy, and set many acres ablaze. But he too got saved, and after that never smoked again. One of our fathers' uncles who claimed to be an atheist was one day trying to pull a loaded trailer up a very steep river hill. The tractor petered out and the rig began rolling back downhill, and Grandpa Ratzlaff overheard his brother-in-law cry out, *O God help!* My dad himself told me that when the crumpled mess came to a halt at the bottom of the hill, the unbeliever had to sit down and roll a smoke to calm his nerves, and Grandpa taunted him, "*Na Wellem* — Well Bill, are you still an atheist?"

I was in my mid twenties and a very green minister when I went furtively into a Winnipeg drugstore one night and bought my first pipe. It was simple rebellion. At first smoking it was all in the ritual and the secrecy — filling, tamping, striking wooden matches, and puffing out streams of smoke. A brochure that came with my purchase promised that if I took good care of the pipe, eventually it would come to feel like an old friend — like comfortable slippers, maybe, or a faithful dog.

And it was true. That pipe, and every one I bought afterwards, never failed to please me, none ever resembled the cigarette butts I'm dumping this morning from ashtrays to garbage can. My favourite "friend" of all is a cherrywood pipe from a small Luxembourg village. I found it one year just before Larraine and I returned from Europe, after I'd hunted in vain through several other countries. Its red-and-black-grained bowl is smooth to the hand, the stem of the pipe curves in a merest hint of Sherlock Holmes, an altogether beautiful smoking device.

The ashtrays are soaking, dishes and utensils drying, Reverend Crouch still praising Jesus. I recall the magazine ads of the 1950s, double-page spreads of athletes endorsing their brands of cigarettes. One had a facsimile in a bottom corner of a doctor's recommendation of smoking as a good way to relax after a strenuous workout or game, like this athlete, his patient, did regularly.

The weather outside the window looks fine. I hang up the dish towel, switch off Andraé's hallabalujah, and step out for a walk to the river.

Many people strolling in the morning air, and how shall I greet them? Suppose they're Buddhist or Jewish or Muslim — would it be wrong to wish them a Happy Easter? So I merely nod in passing, *How's it going?*

An hour's walk burns off some of last night's calories. I sit on a park bench, satisfied with my workout but already thinking of the Luxembourg friend waiting at home, wondering how far my willpower could go in renouncing the *Tabak*.

Here comes a young girl across the ball diamond dragging on a cigarette, looking every bit as cool as I wanted to be at her age. She smiles and says, "Jeez, it's nearly hot out here."

A whiff of smoke hangs on the breeze. I inhale deeply and say, "It's a fine day for sure."

She walks on and exhales another stream, then turns and says over her shoulder, "By the way, Happy Easter."

☾

When I arrived at Jim's house some relatives were visiting him. They quoted biblical texts to see him through his dying time. To me it sounded rote and heartless, but Jim accepted it with grace. When they left, I sat again on the floor beside his couch, and he said, "Lloyd, for me the guilt issue is resolved."

I said, "Then everything's fine, Jim," knowing how for both of us guilt was a rock we pushed uphill every day and by nightfall found it rolled back down.

We talked about memory, peace, childlikeness — everything except driving and hunting. He spoke openly of his death. He said when he gets to heaven he'd like to see his daughter Julie first, then his father, then mine.

"It's a wonderful thought," I said, and asked him to put in a good word for me, to let Dad know that I'm okay.

For the first time in our lives, Bindy kissed my cheek and said, "I love you. I'll pray for your peace."

On a slow and mostly quiet drive home, I suddenly caught myself humming another old hymn from childhood, *Grace that is greater than all our sins.* It had long ago come to sound unctuous, but now it only drew a smile and a tear, and played on in my head through the rest of the day.

☾

I sat on a fat, low fence post along St. Henry Avenue and closed my eyes to let thoughts settle, and inhaled the spring air.

In the distance I could hear a man coming with his dogs, and idly recalled how the Buddha was said to have remained still in the forest even when wild animals approached. I resolved to try my own version of it.

Suddenly the hounds were sniffing at my legs. I opened my eyes and petted them, and from a distance heard the owner call out an apology, "Sorry for the interruption. Looked like you were meditating or something."

I said, "As a matter of fact I was," and assured him it was no intrusion.

As he caught up he laughed, "The dogs never see anyone just sitting," and as he moved on called back, "We should all do more of that."

☾

I've gone to meet Jim at the hospital where he's had an appointment. He walks out through the front door without stumbling and begins running toward his car in the parking lot. I fear that if he plans to drive he'll have an accident, yet his vigour is astonishing.

Suddenly he's elevated high in the air. Thick drops of a liquid dark as blood drip down from him, and a disembodied voice announces that he is very close to death.

At 7:00 AM I'm awakened by a phone call saying that Jim died a few minutes before sunrise. My brother has ascended. *They shall walk and not faint,* says the prophet Isaiah, *they shall run and not be weary, they shall mount up with wings as eagles.*

When we were growing up Bindy was always ahead of me, older, taller, smarter about sex. He was chief of the Moonlight Prowlers, a gang to which I never belonged but once saw their fort in a bush across the field from his farm in the twilight of a summer evening, when he went to fetch a little spiral notebook in which the minutes of the gang meetings were recorded. We spent time together in fields and granaries, in haylofts and dugouts. As adults we became friends closer than many brothers manage to be. We had only one quarrel in fifty years, which was resolved quickly. We camped out together, drank beer, laughed, grieved, and talked by the hour. He repaired my broken gadgets. Always there was music — sometimes gospel, sometimes blues, sometimes rock and roll.

At a skating party for his seventeenth birthday his friends gave him a card:

The good die young, that's what they say,
And if it's true, then it appears
You'll be around for years and years and years.

The doctors were wrong on another count at least. He never did lose the human things.

☾

This morning I woke to the robin who comes every spring to live on the riverbank across St. Henry. The clock said 4:47 AM, and the creature sang so lustily in the dark that I thought it must be clinging hard to its perch to keep from toppling off.

Yet it wasn't the robin that woke me, but another dream.

In the spotlight below the stage of the Laird community hall, I'm speaking to a home town crowd. I open my arms wide and say, "I love this town," but then begin teetering on my feet. The light grows dim, I become anxious as consciousness fades, and without being able to say more, pass out in front of my people.

It was fear that jarred me back to my bed, and to the lively bird across the way.

☾

Today we buried Jim beside his daughter in Salem cemetery across the road from the farm where he grew up. A prairie wind kept us hanging onto our hats and shielding our eyes from the dust.

Larraine and I stood under a pine tree where a dead branch scraped at our faces as a young niece clung to our hands. My ex-wife stood nearby with a group of my relatives. While we adults wept in the wind, Jim's four-year-old granddaughter Karlee played so happily around his casket that we feared she'd fall into the grave.

Sleep then, dear brother, and sweet dreams. Only the physics of presence have changed. Worlds may appear in our vanishings, for "life is eternal, and love is immortal," says the poet Rossiter W. Raymond, "and death is only a horizon, and a horizon is nothing save the limit of our sight."

Later at the luncheon an elderly woman introduced herself as the mother of Jim's colleague who had died a year ago, who so recently had appeared at the foot of his bed. She hadn't known of this and was glad to hear it. Her son, she said, had also visited her in a "vision" (nor would she call it a dream), and assured her that he was all right — that indeed everything was all right.

☾

Why do I walk the riverbank paths?

For magpie's graceful swoop and faintly ridiculous hop. For the rejoicings of red-winged blackbirds, and for ten yellow goslings bobbing behind their mother goose on a cobalt river.

I walk for two gophers in winter belly up on a snowbank and taking the sun. For the blackest cat among verdant greens after a spring rain. For the red fox who waves a tail and vanishes. For a porcupine up a tree and out on a limb on a high summer night, with Brent and I settling on the path under a gibbous moon and waiting an hour for the creature to scramble down and off through the bush.

And I walk for the trees. A low-branched sycamore which I climb beside the path to sing from its branches, *Zacchaeus was a wee little man, and a wee little man was he.* A bush that feeds me buffaloberries as tart as ever childhood's were. A caragana hedge that shoots brown pods at me where I sit reading Keats, watching smoke unfurl from the Queen Elizabeth Power Station across the river and re-form endless patterns on the sky.

I walk for human surprises, too. A high school kid's poem blown by wind into the public domain:

I dreamt as a child
How life would be

With my perfect Job
 In my perfect World
 How I'd be the king of it all
 And I would have things made
 Oh how life deceived me . . .

Best of all, though, is a late night walk after a dinner party with Brent and Ellen, all our legs strong and unbroken, four of us at three in the morning playing hide-and-seek on the riverbank, and me hiding so well that the others give up and I have to go back to seek for them. And when we've found each other again, lying on our backs on a footbridge where the creek meets the river, passing around a mickey of cinnamon schnapps and looking into the stars.

☾

Summer

Marking Time

The Saskatoon Eaton's store was long ago turned into an Army & Navy outlet, and now they're closing shop too. I'm back here like a fourteen-year-old from the village of Laird to see the place once more, estimate speed and angles of the revolving door, jump in and catch my step, and already am delivered to old magic.

Right here beside the door were things my village never knew. Along this wall of rubber boots there used to be a newsstand — never mind the sports and hot rod magazines, but that one issue of *Cavalier* with a woman holding a ball of fluff like cotton candy in front of the place I could barely think of. And then the preacher's son came from nowhere and saw me enjoying myself, and I knew he'd tell his father or mine and mess up all my chances of being saved or baptized.

Past the banister of the worn marble staircase leading down, and to the back of the store where the old escalator sits, wondrous moving stairs that used to rumble behind the elevators, silent now and gone dead, same glass sides for single-file bodies, same wooden slats and rubber rails. We had no moving stairs in the village. And our elevators hoisted scratchy oats into dim, dusty upper regions, and no gorgeous gloved woman sat on a stool pushing at latticed doors saying *Going up please, going down,* looking so sinfully alluring you could practically see her with her gloves off and a fluff ball like the one in the magazine.

A backroom door says STAFF ONLY. Is the manager in? Could he switch on the stairs please and let me go up? Or ride the old elevator that now says SERVICE ELEVATOR ONLY beside the new lift you command with the poke of a button, admit me into the cross-hatched door and crank the handle going up and down, please?

A kid in the room takes me to a supervisor, who shakes her head and says it ain't allowed since the new elevator come, and I say well I'd like to feel the old times again and so forth, and she thinks the office upstairs might make an exception to the rule, who knows, and I say maybe I'll think it over and try some other time.

New shabbiness contends with old magic, and of course this is reality and that ain't. But still I wish the stairs would move, and a woman slip on a pair of gloves and say, come into my elevator please, going up and down, up and down, oh boy, oh boy . . .

((

Dear Jim,

Do you remember when our Sunday school classes sometimes came out here to the cemetery in summers when the church balcony was too hot even for the teachers, and they brought us to sit with our Bibles under the shade of these pines? We were always so close to our dead. Today I'm sitting on a tombstone like that within sight of your grave. Last night falling asleep I heard you call my name. The voice seemed to come from within, but it was unmistakably yours. Where are you, then?

At one end of a long row of relatives lies our little cousin Douglas who was run over by a car before his third birthday. Beside him are the four aunts we never knew who all died in childhood, three in the same year, one at thirty-six days, one at seven years, another just a day short of her ninth birthday, and the last one was stillborn. Next, our Ratzlaff grandparents' headstones chiselled with the same text from the book of *Revelation*: "They overcame by the blood of the Lamb." Then your Julie surrounded by a white chain-link fence, and beside her the fresh mound of earth settling above your body. Stretching out toward the road are the graves of our fathers and uncles, with empty spaces awaiting their wives.

All around in the earth are the bodies we lived with. Surely these ancestors laughed and railed and lusted and knew their ecstasies — then why this overwhelming sense of their gravity and righteousness? I honour them for everything *but* their beliefs in literal gold streets and pearly gates — yet how foolish it sounds now that I say it, for they knew how to wait for rain on parched seeds, how to dig graves for their children with their own shovels.

A small gopher watches intently from behind a headstone. Now it scurries off, stands again like a signpost between two other graves. I get up to follow, and it scampers past more and more plots — Heppner, Grunau, Strobel, a deacon named Earnest August Jeschke — skirting even the entrances to its own underground home, and in another two laps has drawn me to the edge of the cemetery where it vanishes in a green wheat field under the blue vault of the sky.

You haven't gone far, Bindy, but you've become unavailable for my purposes. Still, I can't imagine that you and I are not being remade.

Trust beyond belief, beyond disbelief.

☾

One Saturday in the 1950s an uncle and aunt who were missionaries on furlough from Africa stayed overnight with our family. I was on the verge of adolescence, in awe of their world-travelled and culture-crossing lives. That night after supper my uncle took his Bible to the dining room table and began working on a sermon he was to deliver the next morning in Salem Church, and I looked forward to it with relish and great pride.

My aunt was visiting with Mom in the kitchen while Dad began fixing a tap under the sink. But my uncle seemed to grow more and more edgy, and suddenly he exploded at his wife, "Get in here! Start preparing some lessons! What if they ask you to teach a Sunday school class tomorrow?"

She came meekly from the kitchen and fetched her own Bible, and in the awkward silence I escaped upstairs to my bedroom (I hadn't yet moved to the cellar) and continued working at a correspondence course from a religious broadcast I often heard on the radio. I came to the question, "Who wrote the Bible?" with a blank line waiting to be filled.

I knew, of course, that the Bible had been written by many people — Moses, Isaiah, Matthew, Mark, and Luke — but was puzzled at the question, as if it called for a single answer.

I went back down to the dining room where my uncle and aunt pored silently over their scriptures. Not wanting to interrupt, I went to the kitchen where my father still had his head under the sink and asked him, "Who wrote the Bible?"

His reply sounded like a snort. "Well— don't you know?"

I said no, I didn't. He paused to adjust the pipe wrench, and said, "Well, *God.*"

I went back up and wrote God on the line.

((

Today Brent said, "Lloyd, I'm gonna do like it says in the Bible — if your leg offends you, cut the fucker off." He's still hospitalized with his recurring knee infections, but occasionally now he sounds more like his old self.

He was raised Catholic but never became "Cathaholic" (as another acquaintance labels his childhood religion). By the standards of my upbringing, Brent's was enviably lax. Once he and Ellen took us to visit the Miramachi, and we dropped in on one of his cousins who happened to be recovering from the previous night's adventure and complaining glumly, "Ya have a few drinks, and the next day hafta run all over the jesus country lookin' fer yer hat." I thought what a gift it would have been to people like Jim and me to be allowed something like that and still to feel that we were Christians in good standing. But always there was that old rock of guilt rolling down like the stone of Sisyphus onto our heads.

((

Larraine's work stresses and physical pains haven't abated, and now she's trying also to complete a master's thesis before the fall deadline.

This may be the wrong time for me to quit smoking, but I've taken the plunge.

Why now? Because of a burning in my chest and some strange business in my throat that no lozenges will soothe. Because cancer killed my brother — not that he ever smoked, but the tumours got him anyway.

Once I heard a Yiddish comedian tell about his mother catching him smoking. She said, "You wanna smoke? I'll tell you what will happen. First you'll smoke, then you'll drink, then you'll gamble. Then you'll hold up a bank to pay off gambling debts, and you'll get arrested and they'll put you in Sing Sing, and when you're sitting in the electric chair, *then you'll first smoke.*"

For much of yesterday I paced and puttered, and even prayed though I couldn't imagine a deity paying heed after my long heedlessness. Finally I walked to the drugstore for a pack of nicotine gum to "add power to my will" as a current commercial promises. This foul product diminishes cravings all right, but only by generating one hell of a heartburn to match the other fire in my chest.

Late in the evening I strode to the park, found a calm spot out of the wind, and sat on the riverbank thinking, *Which way I fly is hell; myself am hell.* Now I'm first smoking.

When I got back home Larraine was watching TV. She saw how frantic I still was and said, "I don't think we should talk for a while." To which I retorted, "We haven't talked for a few weeks anyway, so a few more shouldn't hurt." This only made me feel worse, and I could hear the lameness in my apology, "No one can do this quitting for me" (thinking *No laughing Buddha, no bronze beauty, no gnarled stickman regardless of how I kiss his wooden hump).*

I ran a tub and soaked in hot water. Larraine finished watching her show and went to bed. I took her place on the couch and watched the late news, and sometime after midnight fell asleep.

But then it was morning again, and still no power in my will.

☾

One summer afternoon before I turned twelve I was loitering near a caragana hedge in the alley behind the Lutheran Church and the Imperial Bank, from where I could see the side door of Don's Groceteria across the street. I was planning to steal some cigarettes — Vogue cigarettes in particular. I couldn't shake the image of that woman outlined red on yellow, her slender neck and bobbed hair and perfect round earrings, and the painted lips saying, *Look here, Lloyd, men around town carry me in their shirt pockets, hoods roll me where their muscles are.*

But I fretted about the sin. God's eyes were watching, so I crossed the street, went farther down the alley and stood by the garbage barrel behind Dix Hardware. The Eyes were there, too, and I returned to the street and headed down toward Kenny Redekopp's house. But here came George Andres in his blue '51 Chev half-ton, turning in the cab to look sourly at me from behind his thick lenses. He was janitor of the school and the bank, and everyone knew enough to stay out of the way of his brooms. Now for sure he'd see I was up to no good.

I kept walking until he parked at the stop sign beside Don's store and got out of his truck. He carried a mop and pail through the back door of the bank, and I thought again about the woman on the Vogue package and hurried back to the alley to resume my lookout.

An air hose hissed from George Klassen's garage. I fidgeted. Farther down the street a buzz saw whined at the Reliance Lumber Yard.

Then I saw Nickel's Transport turn the corner a block to the south and approach the store until it pulled to a stop behind the janitor's half-ton. This was what I'd been waiting for. Soon Don Regier would be busy unpacking his new shipment of groceries.

Leonard Nickel opened the back of his transport, took out a case of bananas, and carried it into the store. I waited. He came back out, hoisted another crate and hauled it inside. I shot a glance up and down the street, darted across and into the open door and saw Don already at the far wall unpacking the bananas. He never looked around as I sauntered up the aisle, past work shirts and garden sprays toward the school-supply section near the front, from where I had a clear view of the counter. There were the Vogues stacked between cans of Daily Mail tobacco on one side and neat columns of rolling papers on the other.

I watched until Nickel made another trip outside. This time he returned with a carton of meats from Intercontinental Packers. Don followed him to the cooler at the back of the store. No other customers around — *now's* the time — and I scooted behind the counter, a pack of Vogues vanished into my pocket, and I bolted through the front door, around the corner, past the janitor's truck and the waiting transport, past Kenny's house and the village pump, through a ditch and into a poplar thicket where I came to a halt panting like a hound. Never such commotion! Such ripping of cellophane and peeling back of foil!

I steadied my hand to expose the perfect round tips of the Vogues, and tugged one up to make it stand above the others like the magazine ads showed. The woman smiled and her ruby lips dared, *Smoke me, Lloyd, I'm the finest, I'm the smoothest.*

I pulled the tube from the pack and held it to my nostrils — ah, the fragrance that had made me so weak when I once found an unsmoked cigarette in a ditch. I lowered this one to my mouth, let it dangle from a corner of my lips like the men did. I tapped my pocket for matches — and realized I'd forgotten to steal any.

Now God's voice came from the firmament: *You can't smoke them, you thief. You know where thieves go when they die, and tonight may be the very night you die.*

I spat out the cigarette, took two more from the pack and crushed them in my fist. Pulled out another one, and mashed it and threw it to the ground — *nobody* will smoke them — tore off the remaining foil and pulverized every cigarette but the last, which I held for an instant between two fingers like a man, then crushed it too and heaved it after the others so hard I wrenched my shoulder.

The Vogue woman smiled her last as she crumpled in my other fist, then she was gone to the bush too, and I was running back toward the road, out to the edge of town, to the dugout near Adam Schmidt's hut where I came to another dizzy stop.

God was knocking on the walls of the world. How could I go home now and sit at the supper table pretending to have Jesus in my heart?

But it was suppertime, and I had to go home.

☾

In Rodlyn Grunau's farmhouse attic there was an old Oliver typewriter he said was for sale. I knew I could never afford the second-hand Royal portable from Friesen's department store in Rosthern with a carrying case and locking clasp, and would just have to settle for the Oliver. My parents had forbidden me to pay more than ten dollars for it, but Rod held out for an extra buck, and I handed over eleven, glad to finally own a typewriter at all, no matter what lectures would come later.

The machine was a cast iron beast patented in 1896, already fifty years old at the time of my purchase. It needed two strong men and a boy to haul it around, but finally we got it wrestled up to my room and set on a desk Grandpa Gliege had built. With the help of a one-volume home encyclopedia I began poking around the keyboard, which had three — not four — rows of keys, and separate shifts on the left to lever the carriage forward and backward. The letters themselves were mounted on banks of inverted U-shaped steel bars, and when I hit the keys hard enough they slapped down on the roller, punching out little paper circles from the "o"s and "a"s and "9"s.

After I'd acquired a speed of around fifteen words per minute, a Mennonite writer who had been my Sunday school teacher offered me twenty dollars to type a three-hundred-page manuscript of a book she was working on. I was elated, and between school assignments and chores at home I laboured at this project for months, having learned to type with just the right pressure so the words would not be too dim but the pages wouldn't have holes cut out of them. I knew already that I'd rather be a writer of words than a harvester of oats or feeder of chickens.

I was fifteen years old. By that time Jim had already owned two motorcycles without ever wanting a typewriter, and now I had my typewriter without ever having really wished for a motorcycle, though I was glad enough to ride around the country roads with Jim while hanging onto his back.

On that colossus of mine I also typed Grandpa Gliege's memoirs, which he'd handwritten in a careful German script I learned to decipher. I volunteered to type the minutes of Salem Church business meetings, happy to have anything at all to do with words and publishing, which seemed better than shovelling animals' shit and spreading new straw for them to sleep in.

As an adult I did own other typewriters, including a Royal portable like the one I had coveted as a kid; and still later, shortly before the dawn of the computer age, an electric model that astounded me with its speed, so I could type twice as much twice as fast. My old eleven-dollar treasure eventually found a place on an office shelf, from where it oversees my doings to this day.

In the mid-1970s I visited a long-lost cousin in Thunder Bay who operated a business machine store. I discovered that he owned two of these venerable Olivers, and he clearly felt the same about them as I do about mine. One he kept under a glass counter at the front of his store, and the other was packed away in mothballs at home. He had been offered a thousand dollars each for them, but was unwilling to part with either one.

(

One of my Morris Mennonite Church parishioners happened also to be a longtime member of the Toastmasters Club. He had often urged me to join the local chapter, certain that they could help improve my speaking skills as a minister — not that they weren't good now, but, you know, everyone has things to learn.

Eventually I joined. The group convened weekly for a meal in the hotel dining room before getting underway with the speeches, and for several weeks I was allowed to observe others as they honed their skills and pondered criticisms. Then one night I was asked to prepare a brief introduction for the next meeting, merely an icebreaker which would be exempt from the usual scrutiny. And although this assignment was easy, the next one was not.

My turn came to deliver a two-minute impromptu speech on a subject of the toastmaster's choice. These talks were considered after-dinner entertainments, designed to ease the group into the lengthier prepared addresses to follow which represented the club's real business. A topic was assigned, the member composed his speech while heading toward the podium, and the toastmaster sat off to one side with a stopwatch and a panel of green, amber, and red lights. When the green bulb was lit, the talk commenced. At one minute and forty seconds the yellow bulb came on briefly. At two minutes and twenty seconds the red light signalled the group to conclude the speech in any way it saw fit — by thumping, jeering, or if necessary escorting the speaker bodily back to his seat. Even worse was an unwritten law that these talks must be humorous, for every previous speaker had been wonderfully witty, thus proving the old Zen aphorism that laughter is the sincerest form of applause.

After dinner that night the toastmaster took a newspaper clipping from his pocket, unfolded it, and read it out to the group. A certain man had died, we learned, but before his death had recorded a message with instructions that a device be mounted in his tombstone to activate the recording whenever a visitor approached the grave. He would speak to the living from among the dead.

"So come up here, Lloyd," said the toastmaster, "and tell us what you'd like your headstone to say."

I got to my feet. So far, so good.

Walking to the front I had only these thoughts in mind — I have to be funny, yet how can a pastor make jokes about death, and how will I avoid sounding preachy? Then I was at the podium, the green light came on, and I launched into a speech: "If I were to speak to you from the other side — "

For the first (and so far only) time in my life, I blanked out.

Thirty men sat with waiting faces, the toastmaster sat with a thumb poised over his stopwatch, and there was the green bulb, glowing. Later I found it almost impossible to believe the others when they said I had been "gone" for only about twenty seconds. It might as well have been all eternity that passed before I found a voice to mumble some truism about living life as fully as we can while we have the chance. But even this meagre thought had petered out so quickly that I was shuffling back to my seat before the amber light ever came on.

(

Over lunch my daughter Sheri and I had a long discussion about work, stress, marriage, and faith. She and Rob are active members of the Free Methodist Church, and at one point she asked, with no hint of reproach or interrogation, "Do you still hold to any of your old beliefs?"

I recalled a day when she was four or five and we were sitting on the patio of the 8th Street MacDonald's. Suddenly she saw a sparrow hopping over the stones pecking at french fries and said, "There's a bird, I'm gonna hunt for it," and tailed it till it flew off.

I'm sure I must have looked away at the question about my beliefs, but finally said that I try to circle around Christian symbols and imagine them from other viewpoints. That these symbols keep dying and rising again. That belief often seems to me indistinguishable from make-believe (while mere unbelief is too often tempted to say what's impossible in this universe), and that all these "liefs" easily consume energy without regenerating it.

She seemed more comfortable with the response than I was.

On the drive home I remembered a song from a dream, a song I'd never heard before which came with both music and lyrics: *Whatever she saw / she took to the dumpster / to put there whatever / the dumpster was for.* I thought about a clean-out some years ago where I'd discarded thousands of pages of university notes, weary of carting them around every time I moved, and it had felt like a good and healthy enema. I thought also of the hundreds of sermons delivered in my ministerial years — why had I still clung to these relics?

By mid-afternoon I'd found the old files and set up the paper shredder. I began feeding page after yellowed page into the machine, apologizing to everyone who had endured those preachments, and recalled the biblical warning that a record is kept of every idle word we speak. One more gospel tune nagged at me, *O he sees all you do, he hears all you say, my Lord's a-writin' all the time.*

Some of those old words, at any rate, are no longer in my file cabinet. If some universal archive retains them for future reference, what a pity it would be.

Billy Graham's autobiography *Just as I Am* is a journalistic account of his fifty years of world-roving evangelism. Only near the end of eight hundred pages does it take on a more personal tone, where he describes his feelings at having been so far from home while his children were growing up. Two of their sons had "experimental" or rebellious phases, and one daughter is divorced.

Billy is said to have spoken to more people in the world than any other human in history. Popes, presidents, dictators — none has had so huge an audience. What is it about his message that so enthralls the world? *You cain't get to heaven on your own, but Christ died to forgive your sins, now I'm asking hundreds of you to come forward...* And they come, heeding the tireless refrain that he doubtless considers faithful proclamation of gospel truth.

But at the end of his crusades Billy got to pack up and leave town, play golf with presidents or have tea with royalty, while local pastors were left to do what they always did, but now also dealing with the crusades' aftermath, all those hundreds who came up the aisle and got prayed over and were left behind.

I was one of those pastors, once.

☾

A woman was huddled in the bus shelter giving orders to her child who was poking about happily in a grassy patch beside the street: *Don't go there, come here, don't touch that dirty stuff.*

By the time the bus arrived the kid's agenda had been consumed by the adult's, and suddenly he was aware of his "owies." Through most of the ride downtown he fussed and cried, though to me it all seemed contrived; but unable to feign interest in adult concerns over cleanliness and security, and forbidden to follow his own curiosities, he went the only other way he could: into himself and his problems.

I was trying with only marginal success to silence my own mind, and as I stepped from the bus onto Third Avenue an old gentleman looked up from the sidewalk grinning like Hotei back in my living room and said, "Don't speed! There's a cop behind that light pole." He saw me startle and broke into a laugh and added, "But he's only a little fellow."

The old man wasn't drunk, as far as I could see, and I walked away laughing along with this benign mind-police, an *angellos* reminding me to slow down, something I'd already forgotten a hundred times since waking up.

I sat on a sidewalk bench, and another aging man came to join me. We said hello and he lit a cigarette. I was on the verge of expressing envy when he began coughing, and coughed until he doubled over and a dark swill dribbled from his mouth. He spat it to the pavement, and I realized my envy had vanished.

☾

I say Jim is dead only because he's not present in familiar or preferred form. Yet I never did meet the same Bindy twice, as Heraclitus never waded again into the same river. Call life a transfiguration, then, a play of presence and absence where living and dying are one gerunding.

Mel Blanc, who was the voice behind a thousand cartoon characters including Bugs Bunny, Daffy Duck, and Foghorn Leghorn, once had a car accident that left him in a coma for several weeks. As a medical team strove to keep him alive, his family held bedside vigil, but nothing could penetrate his unconsciousness until one day a physician happened to be making rounds as a Warner Brothers cartoon played on the black-and-white television in Mel's room.

On a whim the doctor asked, "How are you today, Bugs Bunny?" From the inert body on the bed came an unmistakable Brooklynese voice: "Eh, just fine, Doc. How're you?"

The astounded physician halted, and asked again, "How about you, Porky Pig?" And Porky's voice answered, "J-uh-ju-uh-just f-fine, th-th-thanks!"

Although Mel himself retained no memory of this, the emergence of these cartoon characters marked a turnaround in his illness, and in his autobiography, *That's Not All, Folks!* he concludes, "I may have been on the verge of death, but Bugs and Porky were very much alive inside me."

For several years of his childhood, my nephew Darcy had recurring night terrors. He looked hideous to his parents as he came down the stairs like a terrified, terrifying zombie, and they completely helpless to rouse him; yet Darcy himself was not "there," either to himself or to his family, for he never remembered a single one of these episodes. At one stage in Eric Clapton's career he recorded a Michelob beer commercial so intoxicated that he never knew about it until later in a rehab centre, when someone pointed it out to him while it played on a lounge TV screen. And the famous Schappell twins, conjoined at the head all their lives, say that they have ways of being absent from each other; both of them go on dates, and both have sex — then the other has to be "away".

Here's a photo of a smiling kid beside his house, wearing a pair of "glasses" bent from a piece of wire and playing a "fiddle" sawn from a rough wooden plank. He had only three or four years of memory from which to construct an identity, whereas the man writing these words has had more than fifty — are we two the same person? And the father who snapped the photo, is he a withered corpse under the sod of Salem cemetery a few steps from Bindy's body, or the inventive father who bent the wire frames to fashion the "glatheth" his lisping son wished for, who sawed the toy violin from a board?

After one of my last visits with my father, as I was leaving I suddenly felt constrained to look into his eyes and say, "I love you." He squirmed and grinned, and replied, "Yeah, we've known that for a long time already." It wasn't until he was underground that he ever said he loved me, but when he said it in that dream, he said it plainly.

Who will say this is not real presence, that the old remembered absence is the real thing instead?

☾

A woman and a dolphin and I are in a pool. At first I'm afraid of the animal — it's so huge — but then the three of us begin leaping, two at a time, from water to air and falling back again. When the two humans are aloft their fingertips touch as if joining mirror images; when the dolphin and a human are in the air their noses brush lightly before separating again. And so the dance goes — up and down, joining and parting, man, woman, and dolphin taking turns.

I wake with a childhood tune playing in my mind: *If your friends are my friends, and my friends are your friends, the more we get together the happier we'll be.*

❦

Brent's medical team has prescribed a taxing exercise program for his knee, and since his second homecoming he's been following it more religiously than I know how to pray. He can flex the damaged leg nearly ninety degrees now, and has abandoned his wheelchair for another pair of crutches. He swears to graduate again from crutches to cane.

He'll remain off work indefinitely. The doctors say eventually the leg should be fused, which would mean among other things that he'd never again be able to sit in an airplane seat. Now he's struggling with what he meant in joking about amputation.

❦

Early Sunday morning, summer 1985, and a small company of patrons has boarded Via Rail in Saskatoon. Settled in my window seat I look back out at the tawdry station at the south edge of the city, my hobo instincts fired, on the way to Winnipeg to visit old friends, *This train she's bound for glory, this train.*

Now the shock of sudden, soundless glide forward. Via hitches up its pants and begins to roll. At the first level crossing the klaxon horn blows *long, long, short-long,* warning other vehicles of our approach, unlike the smooth surge of Air Canada turbofans lifting and flying and leaving white tracks unravelling overhead.

Hey! the train picks up speed, fifty or sixty miles an hour, same velocity at which a Greyhound bus or my Sunbird would run along the highway beside us, but in the bus I could only get up to pee and in the car not even that.

Only a handful of travellers riding the rails today. Behind me I hear a guttural voice at the snack counter and something being heated in the microwave. Now the trainman (as his tag identifies him) delivers two muffins to unseen guests ahead. He returns and sits across the aisle from me and announces, "Smoke time!" A passenger more gregarious than I comes to join him, and they light up together. The trainman launches into repartee you rarely see in flight attendants after they've held masks and hoses to their faces and pointed stiltedly at the several exits to be used in the unlikely event of trouble.

In my childhood, trains were the most powerful machines of all. Pitch-dark locomotive and coal car, string of boxcars for prairie grain, lone passenger coach just ahead of the caboose with its protruding chimney that always made it seem like a cozy shack for the crew. And after winter blizzards there was a gigantic plow ahead of the engine, charging at white drifts and tossing off snow in huge arcs — that was some spectacle, that train, it *dealt* with the elements, disdained seasonless flights over the top of the world where there's only thin air above and vapour below.

The diesel horn wails again, and the trainman returns to the coffee bar. I follow, herky-jerky, and while he pours me a cup he tells how he hates being in the rear coach "because it goes up and down so much," his language peppered with sacred and profane expletives for which he feels a need to apologize after learning that I once was a minister, *'cause this train she's a mighty clean train, everybody ridin' in Jesus' name.*

In my childhood, every Tuesday was train day. Sometimes heading for school through the crocus meadow beside the elevators I'd lay a penny on the track (who had nickels?) for the train to flatten, daydreaming about Pat Hardy and hoping she'd accept the copper as a token of my love. I wanted to linger there where the first crocuses of spring bloomed, where killdeers amazed me every time they tried to lure me from their nests hidden so cleverly on open ground. But then the bell would ring from the school tower, and by mid-morning in the classroom I'd be listening for the locomotive whistle, and at recess tore back over the sports grounds to collect my coins, though I never did summon the nerve to offer them to Pat. And if I didn't have a penny, then an old key from Grandpa Gliege would do, or even a steel washer from my father's workshop — Tuesday's train would turn it into a treasure.

Outside my window the hummocks rise and fall. See the flat fields turning by the cogwheel window where I sit and track my train, this train.

A prairie village slides into view. Whoa — we passed the platform where three additional passengers were waiting in a pickup truck, and the engineer backs up the train to collect them!

I step out for fresh air, and the brakeman (Via Rail has not yet felt the impact of unisex language) strikes up a chat as amicable as his colleague's was. After a while, when the new passengers have been hugged by their loved ones and the pickup is turning back toward the highway, the conductor bellows *ALL ABOARD!* And when we're rolling again clackety-clack toward Melville and Brandon North, I stroll to the washroom to see whether that marvellous sign is still hanging there, and it is.

PUBLIC NOTICE
Spitting prohibited
The rules and regulations
of Via Rail Canada
prohibit spitting in cars
or waiting rooms or on platforms
or other premises of the company
and prescribe as a penalty
for any violation or non-observance thereof
a fine not exceeding forty dollars ($40.00)

I spit in the toilet for the hell of it, and swear a grand oath that rail passenger service is one political cause into whose fray I might be tempted to enter.

Because I'm not always in such a hurry as I often am.

☾

The hardest thing these days is breaking the associations of smoking with many other activities. Writing, for instance, has long been tied to smoke. I loved the pipe's aroma as I sipped coffee and worked over lines and outlines; loved it also while talking on the phone, watching movies, partying with Brent and Ellen, taking Jim for a drive — everything called for a smoke.

No use being nostalgic now when the mind is more battle-ground than playground. No use fondling my Luxembourg friend where it reposes on a stand in a corner of the spare bedroom, feeling sorry for itself for no longer having its fire lit.

In a month of non-smoking I've gained ten pounds, chewed off ten fingernails, and outgrown many of my clothes. There are new twinges and pains, and unexpected shortness of breath when I climb the riverbank — wasn't giving up smoking supposed to *add* to Tigger's bounce, not subtract? A couple of times I've gone so far as to sniff into the perfectly-cured cherrywood bowl, and could easily lose the extra weight by packing the pipe with my favourite *Tabak*, which is why I don't keep an emergency pouch in my house. One day I was so nettled at an impasse in applying for a writing retreat that I exploded, "If you're going to be such a miserable prick you may as well smoke!" But the rage passed, as did the urge, and eventually the problem was resolved.

Most days I still have a dozen cravings, but they're not as imperious as they were and don't last quite as long. I'm aiming for six non-*Tabak* weeks, and maybe the seventh will be a sabbatical from the work of quitting.

Rilke no doubt had something more noble in mind when he said, "Who speaks of victory? To endure is all." But today I recite the line for my own solace.

((

A dozen writers and painters have gathered for a retreat at a northern Saskatchewan lake. Last night I was granted my wish for the sound of rain on a cottage roof. A fine drizzle is still falling this morning, and although walking in rain is not conducive to the act of writing ("pencils and what not," as Winnie-the-Pooh complained), it's very good indeed for what Brenda Ueland terms "moodling."

I unfold an umbrella and step into the forest, startled at once by the red berries nestled among archetypal greens. The camp director says there have been several cougar sightings recently, and we must assume that wherever we go in the forest a wild cat will be watching — though he assures us there's no cause for fear.

Other writers are huddled in their quarters, maybe still asleep. At last night's campfire the discussion concerned nap taking at these retreats. The poet Gerald Hill says he's up to 2.8 naps per day, and everyone else acknowledged that sleep is essential for the "subconk" (in John V. Hicks' happy moniker) to work in peace.

On the dresser back in my cabin a miniature Stonehenge is growing up, and this morning I'm on a hunt for additional rocks to complete it. The candidates must have a proper chunky feel and be firm on their bases. Along with the shapes, it's the *colours* of rainwashed stones that I love — and hardly a dozen steps from the door three are already weighing in my pocket.

Here, so far from the city, I can hear the whipping of ravens' wings, and the birds' clucks and mutters when they're not calling. And even in the rain red-headed woodpeckers are tapping at trees.

Descending through a glade, I see that the greens are brighter for the grey skies above. Beside the path is a sitting-stump, a mossy seat too wet to be enjoyed today though yesterday it was the very throne of the universe and I some kind of king being entertained by a nattering squirrel in the pines.

There are many species of mushroom in the forest, each an "enlarged complex aerial fleshy fruiting body of a fungus," as the dictionary teaches. Then why do some resemble tiny weeping birches with strands hanging in the hundreds, and some ripe brown sunflowers, others petite beige quivers bristling with toothpicks? Here's one upturned and cradling rain. It could be a hummingbird bath — see those wings beating the water, showering the moss carpet below. And how many mushrooms resemble hats? Inverted Stetsons, Mexican sombreros, English bobbies' helmets. There is one discus-shaped mushroom so silky and moist that I blush to touch it. Others are certainly some gnome's sacred utensils — a tiny goblet, a diminutive stone-hued font. Here at the base of a fir are the umbrella-shaped roofs of a toadstool village, the hole under the trunk is the entrance to the gnome's treasure house — couldn't he just pop up and nod at us?

I'm nearing the end of the vale now, where one last mushroom stands in the middle of the path like a menacing ruffed grouse, tail feathers fanned out. It's the guardian of Eden.

The trail turns and begins its descent to the lake. I walk in the rain, partly for the joy of going home. I shift my umbrella to another angle against the rain and remove the stones from my pocket to fondle them. The trail narrows, steepens, and turns to gumbo — there go my heels and I'm on my rear end clutching the umbrella, stones flying off, elbows gouging long trenches in the mud before I come sliding, finally, to a halt.

No broken bones, thank Christ, but now only to get home. I clamber back to retrieve the rocks, slink to the lake's edge and rinse them off, peer straight ahead as I go by the cottage windows where other eyes will be looking out at this passing bedraggled man who never kicked much ass but has plainly fallen on his own.

Inside the back door of my house I prop the umbrella in its corner. Already the new stones are drying. Added to those on the dresser, they'll number a perfect biblical seven, and make the little stone circle complete.

☾

I woke up this morning and felt around for the dream, but didn't bother to record it until later when it returned on an afternoon walk. Along with it came a laugh — memory and meaning arriving together:

I've piled on the top of a flagpole (like angels on the head of a pin) the black leather King James Bible my parents gave me as a high school graduation gift, and the Oxford New English Bible I came to love later as a minister, and on top of both a few pages of my own writing.

For an instant I see them perched up there — then like the walls of Jericho they all come tumbling down.

There's more talk about religion among these artists than I'd have expected (none of it initiated by me). Everyone is sympathetic with my continuing struggle to stop smoking, though no one else has ever considered it a sin.

One woman asked whether I believe in God. I replied that as a philosophical principle of origin and containment, yes; as a mythological character, no. But later I had to revise the statement: as principle of origin and containment, yes; as mythological character, also yes — along with devils and angels and creatures at the bottom of the sea (since as someone has observed, reality is what won't go away when we stop believing in it).

In *The Last Temptation of Christ,* Nikos Kazantzakis has some friars questioning their abbot about a puzzling statement he'd made. "'First came the wings and then the angel.' We never noticed these words in Scripture, Holy Abbot."

The abbot replies that it's because their minds are dim. They open the prophets and see nothing but letters, and letters are the black bars of a prison where the spirit strangles itself screaming. But between the letters and lines and all around the margins is where the spirit circulates freely. The abbot ends, "and I circulate with it, and bring you this great message: Friars, first came the wings and then the angel!"

The first time I saw these words they triggered such an outburst of glee that I could never afterward doubt their virtue. I still come back to them often and find my joy scarcely diminished, for the abbot has scored a direct hit on gravity, bibliolatry, and every kind of slumberous institution.

For the fruit of the spirit is joy . . .

☾

In his *Confessions* St. Augustine asks what it is in the soul that makes it take more pleasure in the recovery of things it loves than in their continual possession.

When Larraine and I first met I was still among the repercussions of divorce, and I asked her how she would characterize a good relationship. She said without hesitation, "It's when you have your own life and participate in another's."

After two weeks with fellow writers, on a roundabout drive home I stop at a marsh a half hour from Saskatoon. The moon is coming up over my left shoulder, dabbling ducks on the water call each other without meaning to call me. Tonight Larraine and I will cook a favourite soup and catch up on each other's lives. I think it will taste like trust.

☾

Larraine is still on summer vacation from teaching, but her master's thesis hasn't left her alone for an hour. She did take a night off to celebrate our ninth anniversary. Brent and Ellen invited us to the Bassment, our jazz club downtown, to hear Gary Martin and the Heavenly Blues Band.

Gary is a nephew of Hubert Sumlin, the blues guitarist, and has gospel music in his bones. Near the end of the show he warned, "I want you to go to church tomorrow, 'cause I know you had some bad thoughts tonight." The band launched into a rousing version of "When the Saints Go Marching In," the horn section came parading around the club until half the crowd was strutting and clapping in file behind them (and Brent waved his crutches from the table), and a happy holy ghost was there.

Earlier someone had said that the trombone player was a priest. As the crowd dispersed he sat alone beside the stage and I went to ask whether this was true. He'd been a pastor, he said, not a priest, and I replied, "Same here." Immediately he began questioning me. "Have you ever broken through to the assurance of salvation? Do you know what it is to be filled with the Spirit?" It seemed strange language coming from a jazz musician, but he went on to complain that too many Christians make it their business to tell others how to live. I said I was well acquainted with this religious language, but mostly wanted to say how refreshing it was to hear an ex-preacher blow such a smoky horn.

It's Sunday morning, and after a late night out I'm a bit rough at the edges. Today the bed will be my church, but I'm not sure it's what Gary meant.

☾

Often my walks take me around the back end of a golf course, over a stretch of ground between a chain-link fence on one side and a steep fall to the river on the other. Not being a golfer myself, I had grown used to tossing stray balls I found back onto fairways and greens for the players to use. Then one day my sons-in-law Ramsy and Rob reminded me that they golfed — why not collect some balls for them?

Thus began a semi-serious hunt, which soon became as intriguing to me as the game seems to its players, a philosophical adventure involving physics, mathematics, and the psychology of a man caught between the game and the hunt.

One thing I've learned: golf balls, like humans, take their own ways. Once in a strip of grass beside the path, four balls lay within a handspan of each other, like eggs in a nest. Some luckless player, I thought, must have aimed four times at the flag fluttering just inside the fence, and each time failed in exactly the same way. Yet considering the names of these little spheres, who could wonder that they stray so far from human intent? Palliser Warbird, Maxfli Revolution, Pinnacle Power Core, Infinity Plus Distance ("Serving Saskatchewan Métis since 1987"). Not even the Mojo always works, for there one lies looking up at me through the quitch of the riverbank. Whether it's the United Steel Workers or Creative Goldsmiths or Cyril and Eunice's 25th Anniversary — no matter who the players or how their balls are named, these orbs remain perverse.

It seems I find more golf balls under overcast skies than in bright sunlight. But if I bring some private hellfire in my mind to the search, scarcely a ball turns up. Some of them are invisible, found only by stepping on them (and who knows how many are already underground). Wherever I go there are actual or potential golf balls. They've become a kind of omnipresence, so that I can't *not* look for them.

Some days the hunt takes me far down the riverbank, and the lower I go the higher I have to climb back, the better for my spine and the healthier for my recovering lungs. Down there where so few humans tread is a favourite resting place for some balls — and who'll tell how many are even farther down the gorge than I care to go.

No matter how many golf balls I find, each one startles me anew — there, so improbably, it lies. My record find is fifteen in an hour. You'd think the air would be a-whiz with them, yet I've never been hit on the head or seen a single spheroid in any airspace beyond the fence.

One day's hunt yielded six balls, all named Top Flite — what are the odds? Another day it was nine, variously named, and I wanted to make it a nice round ten until I recalled Miranda Pearson's poem written near the end of her pregnancy, of finding herself "round as a number 9."

Today out of curiosity I counted all the balls in my collection, and it came to exactly ninety-nine. Maybe this afternoon I'll hit 100, call it par for the course, and give the bag to my sons-in-law. Then I can begin looking for birds again.

Now that I think of it, 99 is a good round number indeed, so I declare the hunt over.

☾

Fall

Saw an Angel Workin' on a Chariot Wheel

Dear Bindy,

This is the Labour Day weekend when you and I traditionally went camping. The "tradition" lasted only three years, and on this blue Monday I stopped at your grave wishing I could bring you with me down here to the North Saskatchewan River, to the place someone (was it you?) dubbed "Ratzlaffville" — a grandiose term, wouldn't you say, for the three shacks still here and rapidly going to ruin.

An oversized steel tractor rim has replaced the stone firepit at which you and I sat countless times. Green metal chairs lie around it at crazy angles, and one is in the creek bed half covered by yellowing leaves. The picnic table is listing hard — one shove would topple it down onto the chair. Next time there's a party here someone will toss it on the bonfire for a wiener roast.

The maple tree at the door of the middle cabin leans with age. It was growing here when our parents farmed this land, when you were an infant calling for the moon, *kahnee-kah*, why can't I have it?

And here is the house that someone built. Poplar shoots in the eaves, bullet holes through windowpanes, badger holes under the floor.

Inside the crippled screen door, an inventory of remains. One ratty blanket hanging from a beam. Stovepipe sticking through the wall with an abandoned swallow's nest inside. Workable mousetrap on a pantry shelf. Functional gas can I can't be bothered to steal. Sardine tin on a windowsill full of cigarette butts and a legs-up wasp; and on the floor, the fallen wasp's nest, a few ceiling tiles, glass shards, and paper blinds covered with dust and fly shit.

Bindy, we were not well instructed in the passage of things, or in how to make love to the world. Our joys were sparse and stolen, hoarded rather than kissed on the fly. We wanted them to stay put, and seeing they did not, we clung to promises that a Lamb's blood would admit us someday to the heaven where the preacher at your funeral said you had gone ahead of the rest of us.

I'd bring you down from there if I could, raise you up from your grave. On one of our last visits you said you hadn't done what you wanted in life. I liked to think that I had, unwilling to be one of those poor souls who the poet E.A. Robinson says "stumbled up to manhood, where they saw too late the road they should have taken long ago." But today I came home, Bindy, and it wasn't home.

Some other night I'll come back and howl at the moon for both of us.

☾

Cattle and horses forage in pastures and stubble fields beside the road to Wanuskewin. Skies and ponds are azure in the clean autumn light.

This is the season of old themes returning: love's bitter-sweetness, arms open wide as the world, bearing the unbearable contradiction of longing to be in time while yet letting time pass.

The sun eases back, trees wait. I wait. I gather together all my memories and all my loves in a duration beyond tense or time. A small heart listens, but it listens indeed.

Last night I stood beside my grandfather's house looking into the sky. The moon hung in an eerie haze, and someone said there was a storm up there. Meteors orbited it at great speeds, then plunged from their cycles burning as they fell. Where they fell, no one knows.

Today, the eyes of the bronze woman are too severe for my seeing, her body too lean for me to fathom how everything has already come from her, wild as an animal, and inscrutable as time.

☾

A new academic term is underway, and I've been invited for a third year to teach Introductory Counselling at SUNTEP (the acronym easier on the ear than its expanded Saskatchewan Urban Native Teacher Education Program). For me this entails a ninety-minute drive each way to Prince Albert and back. Most of the students are urban, as the name indicates, but a few live on reserves from which they have to travel as far as I for these classes.

The morning I arrived, one of last year's students met me in the lobby with a hug. She had once embezzled half a million dollars from a national bank, and served time for it. As a course project, she had assembled newspaper reports and court documents pertaining to her case, and prepared a talk which she later gave to a group of inmates at her former prison. She said completing this project was far harder than the embezzling had ever been.

These students' transparency is one of their greatest gifts, though they scarcely know it. Last year another young woman came to class one morning with two black eyes and towing a small daughter, walking in with her head high but barely able to contain her tears. Still she had shown up — where so many others might have stayed hidden in their rooms.

This year fifteen women and three men are enrolled in the class, all in their final year of an education degree. They broke the ice as soon as I entered the room. "Hi, I'm Lorna," one said, "I'm an alcoholic," and burst into laughter. Another said, "I'm Violet and I'm codependent," and everyone laughed along. One young man who looks more African than Native piped up, "My name is Tony and I'm bisexual," and the group roared again. Later during the formal introductions Tony said he did feel marginalized on at least two counts, his mother being Native Canadian and his father African American (but how effortful the labels sound).

Many of the students spoke freely and personally, though a few recited only surface facts of their lives. Two are going through separation or divorce. One middle-aged man was suspicious of this white guy coming to teach, and asked whether I'd ever attended a sweat lodge. I was glad to say I had, that it was the SUNTEP director's own lodge, and the experience had greatly enriched my understanding of therapy.

For an hour we discussed our previous experiences with counsellors. Every one they reported was negative. One woman had consulted a prominent psychologist after separating from her husband, then briefly reconciling and splitting again. As she was pouring out her heart the shrink interrupted: "During the time you were reunited, did you masturbate?" She said she got up and walked out, and I thanked her for making the point better than I could have. I acknowledged some dismal involvements of my own with professional therapists, but when I asked, "Did any of you ever have a good experience?" there was only silence.

I hope this course will remove some of the mystique of counselling, and these students' bantering is already an instance of it, laughter being good medicine and maybe the best. My role will be to ponder their words — groping or determined or broken as they may be — and respond in ways that embody the very "connsolling" (as one woman pronounces it) we're here to learn. It makes grading difficult, but I detest the sham of scribbling a word here or there in the margin, adding a few check marks, and entering a number at the top. In this kind of class, above all others, grading by numbers feels like painting by numbers.

Carl Rogers was the psychologist who first inspired me to expunge as much competition from education as possible. Good (or even half-decent) therapists don't measure one person by another, just as Emerson refused to fault a rose outside his window for failing to be like former or better roses. If teaching must become a judgement, I'll have lost interest in being a teacher.

((

Beneath its posturings, fundamentalism is driven by the very fear it professes to dispel. It starts out with slogans for what, if anything, should be sums to a life. It can obscure the vision of

Bible-thumping revivalists, no doubt, but also of otherwise-alert Catholics who say "when the Pope speaks I stop thinking" or of gifted graduate students who reject ideas out of hand "because they go against my born-again beliefs." Fundamentalism can stunt development, overrun schools, elect governments, and too often imagine itself a righteous remnant against the stinking mass of humanity, even half wishing for Armageddon — let's all die so we chosen few can go to heaven.

It's a Wizard of Oz story. The child, scarecrow, cowardly lion, and tin man all believe the wizard has some potion to get them home to Kansas. But he only frightens them with smoke and noise, and the real magic concerns waking up from the dream, which resolves all the lostness, cowardice, and heartlessness (though no one in Kansas or Oz can prevent the next twister).

My adventure has taken me far from doomsday religion and its cynical philosophy. I have abandoned any "faith" construed as assent to dogma or as blind existential leap. Still, my tradition gave me a taste for the sublime and none whatever for warmongering or professional boxing — then how can I be ungrateful?

As for any heavens I may crave, one anonymous medieval mystic said: "Heaven ghostly, is as high down as up, and up as down: behind as before, before as behind, on one side as another. Insomuch, that whoso had a true desire for to be at heaven, then that same time he were in heaven ghostly. Be wary that thou conceive not bodily, that which is meant ghostly, although it be spoken bodily in bodily words as be these, up or down, in or out, behind or before. This thought may be better felt than seen; for it is full blind and full dark to them that have but little while looked thereupon."

☾

Chuang Tzu's butterfly dream:

> Once upon a time, I, Chuang Tzu, dreamt I was a butterfly, fluttering hither and thither.
>
> I was conscious only of following my fancies as a butterfly, and was unconscious of my individuality as a man. Suddenly, I awoke, and there I lay, myself again. Now I do not know whether I was then a man dreaming I was a butterfly, or whether I am now a butterfly dreaming I am a man.

When I was a young husband, father, and minister, a year-long series of angry dreams began dismantling the snug notion I had formed of my identity. Back then, any corner store I walked into had paperback books promising to decode any of a thousand dreams in less than a minute — and if only it had been so easy. But there was nothing like the spate of books available now, with therapeutic, scholastic, aboriginal, materialistic, and metaphysical themes. What has not changed for me, however, is a conviction that it's better not to understand these visitations than to misunderstand them. Carl Jung said that whatever the hermeneutical challenges, dreams should be regarded at the very least as experiences the psyche has actually had.

☾

On the day of my funeral a hearse is parked inside the auditorium where the service is to be held, obstructing the flow of people arriving. I shift the car into neutral and let it roll out of the way to accommodate the traffic. Near the front, my casket is resting on a trolley, but suddenly I know I can't imagine myself lying still inside it throughout the ceremony.

An usher glances at the coffin, then grins at me and begins wheeling it from the room. He can see very well that there'll be no funeral.

I go onstage to apologize to the audience, explaining that I don't know how to play dead when I feel so alive. "Dying is no big deal," I declaim, but this sounds too bold and I qualify it: "Well, maybe it's a momentous change." This still sounds wrong, and I see it would be better simply to shut up.

And when I do, all the people go home.

☽

For much of one school year I was asked to counsel a fourteen-year-old boy (I'll call him Blake) who was physically mature and bigger by far than most of his peers, yet awkward and crude and in constant trouble at school. His alcoholic father had abandoned the family long before, but only after inflicting much violence on them; and Blake had endured further ills including sexual abuse from a volunteer in an agency designed to help kids like him. His mother had moved often, and eventually joined a religious sect that operated its own academy which Blake had attended for four years. There he was often strapped for infractions like refusing to raise his arms when hymns were sung in chapel, and he had fallen far behind academically and grown angrier as his environment became more suffocating.

When we met, he was enrolled in another school but still preoccupied with the dark sides of life — fighting, drinking, plotting revenge. I wondered how often he had been cajoled, bribed, even threatened with God's wrath, but after only a few meetings I was already tired of his endless tales of battles and thefts and midnight rambles, and one day said, "I'd like to ask you something maybe no one's asked before. Can you remember any dreams you've had lately?"

The flash of recognition in his eyes was followed by immediate dismissal: "Yeah, but it was just stupid."

I said, "Well, tell me anyway."

He began reporting a long and frightening dream of bears chasing him through the woods, until he found a house and took refuge. There he opened the fridge and found a corpse stuffed inside, and without warning the owner turned hostile, and Blake ran out again through the forest until he found a road and hailed a passing car and made his getaway.

This reminded him of other dreams, especially one of a dark angel who came to terrify him — and as he tried to describe it, so many other things came to his mind that the themes grew intertwined and confusing, but now I knew that I'd gained access to his interior.

Over the next few months, several times a week we discussed his days at school, his nightlife at the arcades, and more and more frequently also his dreamscapes. An astounding cast of figures came to visit him at night: human-sized dogs, snakes on flying carpets, kidnappers, animals following him around. The situations were just as diverse and graphic: running through fires, drowning in green acid rain, winning at a casino but never getting paid, being swept down a sewer toward whirling fan blades at the end.

But there was another, and very different, group of dreams in which he found himself performing kind deeds, like helping an old blind man find a door, or piloting a ship over the ocean to rescue drowning souls. Each time he reported a dream he'd ask, "So what does that mean?" and I'd reply, "I don't know, but try to keep it in mind." I was hoping he might come to feel these experiences as questions to himself: What *does* it mean that sometimes I run like all hell is after me, and other times can't stop myself from helping people in trouble?

One week he dreamt of a small white bird in a garbage can in his alley on the verge of freezing to death. He took the creature home and revived it, and the following week when we met he said the bird had returned to perch on his shoulder with a tiny bell in its beak, and jingled it in his ear.

Around the middle of the year, one day I said, "I think it would be a shame if the only Blake others ever saw was the one who boozes and swaggers and fights, and they never got to meet this other one who's so thoughtful and kind." I reviewed how he'd been forced to memorize Bible texts in the school where they knocked him around, but was willing to bet that Christ could just as well have told another parable — the realm of heaven is like a mustard seed, or a buried treasure, but also like this guy Blake, who can't manage to be so bad that all the good in him gets lost. He seemed stunned at the thought.

The year remained rocky for him to the end, but it had its smooth stretches, too. He befriended a boy in the first grade who suffered from cerebral palsy, helped him up the hill at recess when the slope was icy, read to him daily during the French class from which Blake was exempt. At his eighth grade graduation he was given an award for the work he'd done with this child, and he stood on the auditorium stage unable to hold back his tears.

After he'd been in high school for some months, the new staff said that on all counts he was doing better than anyone — including me — would have predicted, and I recalled Emily Bronte's lines, "I've dreamt in my life dreams that have stayed with me ever after and changed my ideas; they've gone through and through me, like wine through water, and altered the colour of my mind."

❨

Near the end of the SUNTEP class I glanced down and noticed that my bottom shirt button was undone. I fastened it hastily, embarrassed to have displayed my belly to all those women and men, and someone said, "Look, he's turning red!"

I could only think to reply, "See, I'm not a white guy after all" — adding that we Mennonites are actually kind of pink.

Though we're only a month into the term, one student said, "In other classes our professors try to pump things into us. This class evokes, and it always ties everything together." And if this wasn't gift enough, someone else added this tenet of aboriginal philosophy: *The path has infinite patience.*

Driving back to Saskatoon I take a country road (for the road less travelled is also the road less busy), and a few miles south of St. Louis stop at a bend in the South Saskatchewan River, step out of the car to take in the prairie air. This is the land of living skies, as our provincial license plates say, and here the winds whisper, moan, and howl — are they not also living beings, as the elders say? I invoke this autumn sun, dance the middle of the road — how absurd I'd seem to my students, and I feel my face redden again, no native elder for sure, but not a white guy either.

Near Batoche I pass a farmyard where a little Black Sambo sawn from plywood stands at a roadside mailbox, as if saying, *Yassa, I'se gwine fetch de mail fo' y'all.*

❨

In a hut beside the dugout at the edge of Laird lived an old man named Adam Schmidt. He was not Mennonite, despite the surname, and moreover he had a reputation as a water diviner, something that in my mind carried sinister if not evil connotations. Although he lived only two blocks from my childhood house, I can't recall ever seeing him until the day I was five or six when Grandpa Gliege asked him to help find water for a well he planned to dig.

Adam Schmidt wore a huge handlebar moustache like no other in the village, and the morning he came to Grandpa's yard with a willow wand I stood watching, fascinated, as he roamed an area between the house, summer kitchen, and car shed, and although his great moustache occasionally twitched, his willow stick did not. Adam Schmidt sounded very sure of himself when he said, "*Gibt kay Vota*" — it gives no water here.

But Grandpa believed there was water, and decided to dig anyway. Several days later when the well was half dug, Kooney Koenig the drayman delivered a load of timber for the crib, and again I was transfixed as he commanded his huge horses — *Gee! Haw!* — backing them toward the spot Grandpa had chosen between his chicken coop and summer kitchen, and I marvelled how the beasts obeyed those two syllables. Adam Schmidt was on hand again to observe, but again shook his head, and from beneath his moustache repeated, "*Gibt kay Vota*."

There was water. Grandpa covered his well and erected a pump, but the first time I took a drink from it I nearly threw it up. Never had anything tasted so bitter or foul. The water from the village well I usually drank was cold and sweet, and even old Billy Zulauf's well closer to my home had tolerably good water, but I was scared of the man as he strolled about his yard in a black sweater spitting tobacco juice when I passed by with my pail. This water of Grandpa's — if I'd had the capacity to blaspheme I'd have said the rich man in Hades himself would have turned up a nose at it.

Grandpa's poultry flock, however, didn't seem to mind it. Every year a new batch of chicks would arrive by train from Early's Hatchery in Saskatoon, cheeping loudly in cardboard boxes with little ventilating holes, squirming as we lifted them out and dipped their beaks in the water before loosing them under the shield of the brooder stove — how they skedaddled after being confined in those tiny cells. The grown birds, too, drank Grandpa's water without protest (yet how would I know — maybe that's why the roosters were so malevolent whenever I passed through the fence, as if their water supply was all my fault).

Here's what had happened. In one sense, both Grandpa and the diviner were right. The well did not actually tap a water vein, but merely some mineral-infested seepage from a good underground flow elsewhere. Until the day Grandpa died, the year I left high school, I never could drink his water without quailing.

There was a Hallowe'en night when some of us boys snuck along a dark trail between Adam Schmidt's house and the dugout. We were not planning to play tricks or beg for treats, but had gone there to spy. In the dark of that fall evening the wizard's hut seemed hardly the size of my dad's workshop, and from a distance we watched through the kitchen window where he sat playing solitaire by the light of a kerosene lamp. I had never understood how Grandpa could have solicited his divining skills without violating some religious dictum. Besides, hadn't we been taught that playing cards was a sin, the face cards especially holding dark meanings — the joker was the Devil, and to fool with his deck was like playing with our souls.

Adam Schmidt sat at his table, the immense moustache now quite still, and like the old man in a Robert Frost poem I'd discover much later, "A light he was to no one but himself / Where now he sat concerned with he knew what." My grandfather no doubt also knew what he knew, perhaps at that moment was making evening rounds in the chicken coop, gathering late eggs, and seeing his flock to roost.

I know only this much, that in the business of finding water the village diviner was more right than wrong, a most benign joker in our pack.

☾

The academic committee overseeing Larraine's master's thesis has awarded her a "High A," and considers it a model for future graduate students. This completes her program, and also qualifies her for a higher salary bracket as a teacher.

To celebrate the triumph she invited Brent and Ellen to go out with us for dinner. Over the meal we discussed what we should do later. As there seemed to be no general will, I suggested we stop at Bud's for some blues. Larraine said she didn't care one way or another, Ellen didn't want to go if the rest of us didn't want to, and Brent said he was willing to go if everyone else felt like going.

So we all went home instead.

☾

There's a new flicker of hope for Brent. One of Larraine's colleagues had provided a contact for a Toronto surgeon who thinks it may be possible after all to give him an artificial knee.

Today Brent and I celebrated the good news by driving to Asquith, a village a half hour from the city, and it's been many months since his face showed such colour and his spirits were so light. We shot a few games of pool in the hotel, then sat over a pitcher of beer discussing our childhood homes. He's lonely for the Miramichi, and when I think how healing the prairies are for me, I know why he may need to spend time in his home and native land to help cure these dogged infections once for all.

We were about to leave the pub when four locals called us to their table. This is not something Brent can refuse (his Maritime sociability's all intact), and he's fond of playing "six degrees of separation" whenever he meets someone new. Within a few minutes he'd learned that three of the men knew certain people he knew, and the fourth had already heard indirectly about his broken knee.

I was sitting beside a drunken toothless man who was full of redneck comments, and wasn't enjoying his company much until he mentioned that he knew the people who had operated the transport in my hometown when I was a kid. He had worked for many years at the city stockyards where our farm animals were taken to market, and remembered how Leonard Nickel used to wash out his truck before going on to pick up groceries from the Shelley Brothers' warehouse to take back to our stores in Laird.

In turn I told him about the day I snuck into Don's Groceteria when the transport arrived to steal the Vogue cigarettes for which I'd had such youthful lust. But it wasn't until Brent and

I were halfway home that I realized not once through all the afternoon had I craved a smoke.

☾

My mother turned eighty at her last birthday, and today she sounded weary on the phone. Her garden was too much for her this year, she said, "because it bore so terribly."

A few minutes later she called back to apologize for her error. "When I called you I said my garden *bore* so terribly, but what I meant was it *yielded* so terribly."

☾

The SUNTEP students are attending a conference in Saskatoon, and this evening they invited me out to dinner. At the restaurant some of them were embarrassed at not knowing which fork to use, or what orzo soup was, and the conversation remained unusually subdued. At the end they refused to let me pay for my meal — they had invited *me*, they said.

On our way to the door, one of the young women gave me something her father had written. I had met the man briefly one day after class while he was waiting to take his daughter for lunch. His coil-bound booklet is titled *The Way God Leads*, and it recounts his conversion and spiritual history. It's inscribed with a personal note:

> Interesting" when I saw you, I felt something. And always
> wonder why. Hope you enjoy the book.
> Your friend Noel.
> P.S. "God" love's you.

☾

The band was cooking, but no one in the bar would get up to dance until a large man with a name tag dubbing him "John Candy" went onstage and began turning ridiculous maneuvers and contortions, and kept it up until he had the crowd laughing.

I was sitting with two former graduate students deeply involved in a discussion of psychological theory when Mr. Candy began dragging others to the floor. And all his antics were very funny until he came back and circled our table and pounced on me.

"I can't dance," I said, in a fresh grip of Mennonite reluctance, but he manhandled me to the floor and ordered, "Have fun with it!"

Before I knew it, I was prancing with the others, and when Candy left to hunt up fresh prey, two women triangulated me into a dance with them. I turned suddenly shy again and protested, "I don't know how," and one of them said, "Do you think we give a shit?"

So we began circling each other in little Ptolemaic cycles and epicycles, and in my mind I heard a character from some forgotten novel saying, *women are gentle fruitful presences, interpolated among our guilts.*

When I sat down I was wiping sweat from my brow, and my colleagues cheered, and it seemed that maybe sometimes a Mennonite *can* dance after all.

❨

Shannon and Ramsy and two-year old Katy are visiting from the Okanagan for Thanksgiving. Katy and I spent an afternoon together while her parents went on a date and Larraine was working at school. For the first while we played together on the living room floor and coloured some pictures, then I began reading stories to her.

After each book I'd take her to the fridge to pick out a "freezie," which she did one colour at a time before we went back to the living room for the next story. After I read *Billy Goats Gruff*, she wanted me to read it again, and now also asked for two freezies.

Then it was two little popsicles at a time, and she grew ever more enthralled with the goats and the troll. I'd come to the last page — "Snip, snap, snout, this tale's told out" — and already she was gearing up to command, "Again!" I must have reread the book at least a dozen times.

After many trips to the fridge I suspected she had reached, if not surpassed, her quota, and in a tone I hoped was congenial said, "I'll give you one more freezie."

Then we nearly came to loggerheads. She looked evenly at me and said, "I WANT TWO!"

I pondered a moment, and gave in.

This morning when she and her parents were leaving for Kelowna, I sat down at the door to be at eye level with her. We had given her a few suckers for the trip, and I said we wouldn't be seeing her again for a very long time. She clutched the suckers in one hand and reached for the doorknob with the other and said, "Well, goodbye."

☾

I could hear only Larraine's side of the telephone conversation, "Okay . . . Okay . . . Right . . . Okay," twenty or thirty times, right and okay.

But when she hung up she was shaking. Her physician was reporting the results of an MRI. The distressing symptoms have had nothing to do with shingles, but with multiple sclerosis, and many lesions are visible in her spine and brain.

How will I comfort this woman I love?

"Now there's glory for you," Humpty Dumpty says, but he really means, "Now there's a nice knock-down argument for you."

Hotei smiles in his corner — belly, beads, and boatful of light. The gnarled manikin lies prostrate still.

☾

Forgiveness cannot be either mere belief or mere forgetting, but it comes with re-creation. When I rewrite the past, I discover that I have released it, whether through deeper understanding and commonality with others, or by a reconfiguration of gestalts, or through tears that melt barriers of ice.

A sudden pang of love for Salem Church. She was a grace that taught my heart to fear, but not knowing how to relieve that fear drove me to the mystics who helped make sense of human notions of deity.

Meister Eckhart: "Some simple people imagine they will see God as if he were standing yonder and they here. But it is not to be so. God and I: we are one." As for the fantasy of some external deity, this he calls "a ghost you must get rid of."

Hermes Trismegistus: "God is an infinite sphere whose center is everywhere and whose circumference is nowhere."

Angelus Silesius: "When God encloses me he is my circumference; when I enclose God he is my centre."

Plotinus: "For everyone hath all things in himself, and again sees all things in another, so that all things are everywhere and all is all and each is all, the glory is infinite."

And in Teilhard de Chardin's *Prayer of the Universe* I am given an axiom to replace that grisly dogma of substitutionary atonement: "The truth about our position in this world is that in it we are on a cross. The Cross is the symbol of the arduous labor of evolution — rather than the symbol of expiation."

☾

In the hard times after my divorce, separated from the church and most of my kin, one day I came out of the liquor store on 20th Street and saw a man arriving to panhandle on the sidewalk. His legs had been cut off above the knees, and the stumps of his thighs were cushioned by thick felt pads on which he shuffled along as he held out a cup for spare change.

I passed him by without donating, but as soon as I drove off regretted my hardness of heart. I had my bottle, he had none. Was he planning to get drunk? So what — who could he hunt down on those two pitiful stumps? That evening my cocktail tasted flat, and for many a day I was troubled by the man without legs.

One afternoon some months later I was given a second chance. Heading home from work through the 20th Street traffic, I saw the legless man again toiling up the sidewalk toward the liquor store. I pulled over and got out and said, "Man, it looks like you could use a drink. May I get you something?"

He beamed and said, "Thank you, sir, just a bottle of Branvin please."

A cheap sherry with high alcohol content — I knew this from having bought one or two Branvins myself in those first broken-down months when I had looked so desperately for ways to cushion my own pain. Entering the store I deliberated whether to offer him a ride home as well, but felt that neither gesture amounted to anything.

When I came back out I did offer the ride, which he accepted gladly. I held open the passenger door and he hauled himself deftly into the seat. He lived only three blocks away, he said, and on the short drive I asked how he had come to lose his legs.

"Oh," he chuckled, "a train ran over 'em and sliced 'em clean off." Privately I wondered about the details, but already he was pointing at a house ahead and to the right. I stopped at the curb; he tucked the brown bag under his arm and opened the door, lowered himself briskly to the sidewalk and fished for something in his pocket. He held out a business card and said, "God bless you," and turned toward the shabby house set at some distance from the avenue. He never looked back.

I watched him stilter up the stoop, Branvin in hand, toward the side door where a narrow staircase led to his room above.

Pulling into the traffic I glanced at the card. On it was a text from the King James Bible, John 3:16, the one verse which above all others had been branded on my childhood mind: *For God so loved the world* (a horn blew to hurry me along) *that he gave his only begotten son, that whosoever believeth in him should not perish, but have everlasting life.*

And God, I supposed, must have loved the world so much that he also made Branvin, that whosoever loseth a pair of legs might not suffer forever, but sometimes have maybe an hour or two of joy.

❨

Larraine and I are at an MS conference to learn more about this disease so frightening to her and still so baffling to medical science.

The keynote speaker is a thirty-two-year-old professor of kinesthesiology. He begins by saying he just hates microphones, he simply has too much energy to stand in one spot. Indeed, he roves the stage with a portable mike sharing his passion for fitness, seemingly unaware that most of the audience has arrived on wheelchairs or scooters or hobbled in on the crutches lying beside them in the aisles.

Practically no one among the professor's two hundred auditors has the "optimal fat-to-muscle ratio" that so enthuses him — he may well be the only one who's got it right. He emphasizes his points with double whammies: *pragmatic-practical, extended-prolonged, ambulatory-upright, fundamental-basic.* Some things he *extrapolates out,* and he speaks confidently *from a movement standpoint,* and even *from the standpoint of minerals.*

Larraine and I shake our heads, grope for each other's hands.

At home I look up the word kinesthesia. The dictionary says: *more at anesthesia.*

((

The SUNTEP students say that in aboriginal tradition first cousins are siblings, uncles and aunts are step-parents, and elders are grandfathers or grandmothers. In that case Bindy and I, being double cousins and soul brothers, are fraternal twins.

When he was dying, he sometimes seemed almost as forlorn at being unable to drive as he was over his cancer. In our teens, I was the thrilled younger brother riding with him in his family's 1956 Buick, the green liquid speedometer bar buried past a hundred and twenty miles an hour (no kilometres in our country) along gravel roads between the North and South Saskatchewan Rivers. He drove like that in broad daylight heading for town to pick up parts for some broken farm implement, and on dark nights after Salem Church's youth groups blowing off steam, with maybe a pit stop at Voth's Service for a buck's worth of gas to bring the gauge up to empty. Once he took a G-6 Minneapolis Moline tractor from his farm out to the Blaine Lake highway, and above the river hill shifted into neutral and coasted all the way onto the Petrofka Bridge, waving at a car he passed on the way down.

It's a miracle he survived as long as he did.

There were two horses at Jim's farm, Roger the high-spirited one, and Jack, older and slower, who was my usual mount. One day we were out riding and Jim stopped along the correction line two miles from the farm and offered to trade horses. I was scared, but reluctantly agreed. He hopped onto Jack's back and galloped off while I tried bravely to urge Roger forward. The beast balked for five minutes before he was willing to go, but when he went there was no stopping him. He streaked for home as my legs clung to his back and my arms hauled uselessly at the reins, and at the last second swerved into the Salem churchyard where Grandpa Gliege was repairing Grandma's grave in the cemetery. Roger headed full tilt for the fence and stopped an inch away — I catapulted over his head like a pole vaulter and landed on my feet inside the cemetery with the reins still in my hands. Grandpa gawked, and I tried to "do as if nothing was" (as Mennonites say), as if I had ridden and dismounted this way many times before.

I remember the high places at Bindy's farm. The windmill our fathers and uncles raced up and down in their youth, which

Jim did just as nimbly but I attempted only rarely. The hayloft in the barn with two ladders against the back wall leading up to wooden apple crates near the peak where pigeons brooded on their eggs — how I prayed the birds wouldn't fly out at my head when I checked their nests for babies while clinging to rungs a thousand feet in the air. The "tree house" (really just a platform in a poplar) to which I mounted on scraps of lumber nailed to the trunk, and hauled myself over the edge and collapsed in a heap praising God I'd made it once more without plummeting to my death.

Jim is in a crew helping to move my adolescent house into the city. I see the rig come rounding a corner between St. Paul's Cathedral and the Sheraton Cavalier Hotel. The house has been painted a light, restful green, and the veranda I loved as a kid is intact and sturdy. Jim has attached a plush leather seat to one side of it, and he assures me that I'll find the rest of the trip very comfortable.

☾

The university term is ending too soon. I met individually with the SUNTEP students to discuss final grades. One woman "knows for sure" she's destined for the counselling profession. Another cried in saying how the class has changed her. The oldest student, a woman from a northern reserve, has renewed her resolve to write children's books. And the beauty who resembles the Wanuskewin bronze turned shy and tearful saying goodbye.

When I think how callow I was at the beginning of my career, I can only wish these students to be spared my blunders while hoping they'll come to know some of my joys. Evaluating them at all seems arrogant, and I'd like to tell the department head that everyone in the class gets an A+, even if it means I never teach again.

Dear Friends,

Grading has always troubled me, most especially in a class like this where we're learning to be honest with ourselves. I could give you a million points for your work and consider it more accurate than the tidy range of numbers I'll have to submit to the registrar's office. I see how deeply you've searched within yourselves, and feel lucky to have been involved, however briefly, with your adventures.

Carl Jung once dreamt that he was in his garden with a hoe. At one spot a stream of water rose from the ground, and with his hoe he was digging a trench to lead it to another place where it went underground again. When he woke, he knew at once that the dream was an image of psychotherapy, and that his life's work was to channel emerging waters back toward the depths from which they sprang.

I've included a few lines of individual response to your projects, which I return to you with my thanks and admiration. And I offer you this thought from one of my many mentors: a pupil who remains a pupil serves the teacher but poorly.

☾

The doctors have categorized Larraine's multiple sclerosis as relapsing/remitting, a medical way of saying that the symptoms seem to come and go. She's begun a costly drug treatment, subsidized in part by health plans, which cannot be considered a cure but is thought to diminish both the intensity and the frequency of episodes, thus retarding the impact of the disease over a projected lifetime. Still, the implications remain unknown; the effects of MS range widely among permanent and temporary disablements, including blindness and paralysis.

What is the sound of one cedar rubbing against a board fence in the October wind?

It's the sound of them speaking in their own tongues.

☾

I sat in a chair in the farmyard where Bindy's father and mine, Bindy too, had been raised. The wooden two-storey house still stood, but the yard around it was only a small clearing now, for over the years a thick brush had grown up, and from where I sat it seemed the trees on the north side of the house nearly touched the roof.

Under a tree nearby my paternal grandfather sat in another chair, looking quietly at his old home. The poplars rustled in the breeze; otherwise the only sounds came from deep in the bush where many male cousins were beating the undergrowth with dogs, hunting for a fugitive who was said to be in the vicinity.

The men came to circle the farmhouse, then returned to the bush, but the fugitive continued to elude them, and finally they gathered in an upstairs room of the house to confer. When they came down again, four of the cousins had been left posted as lookouts at the upper corner windows. The rest whistled for their dogs and resumed the hunt.

Suddenly a small furred animal emerged from a thicket at the east and began timidly to cross the clearing. A guard on the housetop saw it and sent the dogs in pursuit, and others from the bush yelled, "Shoot it! Shoot it!" The creature darted ahead— and now in the strange way of the dream was transformed in a heartbeat into a ravishing beauty running toward me holding a gift in her outstretched hands. I was on my feet when she stopped before me panting from the chase, and the men at the edge of the yard fell silent and all the hounds slunk back. The woman embraced me, and now I remembered an ancient story promising that one day this being would turn out to be myself, and I could only murmur in her ear, "I don't want this bond to be an ordinary one."

Then, in that strange dream's way, the fugitive who had been both animal and goddess changed again, and stood before me, a thick-ankled matron appearing so very ordinary that I was startled awake.

What was the gift she carried?

Ah, if only I knew. But when I fell asleep again, I found myself in a vast cathedral where white-robed figures came streaming from the aisles into a central nave, and stood silently facing each other with white tapers burning in their hands.

☽

It was an October afternoon. I was flying to Albuquerque in a joyful mood, headed for the Pecos Benedictine Monastery where Morton Kelsey and John Sanford, two Episcopal priests and Jungian analysts, were to conduct a week-long retreat in depth psychology and spiritual life.

I had been raised, in Eugene Rolfe's phrase, to be "house-trained but not world-worthy," and after being booted from my village compound (Joseph Campbell's term for a *status quo*) I wandered in an emotional jungle where Carl Jung had appeared as one of Campbell's mythical helpers to show me a means of survival. And later when I began working as a therapist for troubled children, Jung's psychology lent professional aid and comfort as well; but this conference for which I was registered would be my first meeting with Jungians in the flesh, and no excursion had ever seemed more welcome.

After a brief stopover in Salt Lake City, we had taken off again for New Mexico. Twenty minutes into the flight I found myself grinning at a Bugs Bunny voice in my head, *Shoulda toined left at Albukoiky,* when the pilot began his announcement.

"Good evening, ladies and gentlemen, this is the captain speaking. Thank you for flying Western Airlines today. We've reached our cruising altitude — "

And without warning the plane began to shake, as if some great angry beast had come roaring around us, making the pilot break off in mid sentence and the ice cubes rattle in our drinks.

Are we going down?

Passengers glanced nervously at the crew members who kept bustling fore and aft, eyeing each other, too, but remaining silent.

Now a flood of images. My adolescent daughters — how will these two sweet ones fare? My estranged partner and our impending divorce. My parents who had long feared for my soul's salvation. A fourth-grade girl in my counselling room who always drew pictures of disasters, things going up in flames or down, and will this plane come apart, will we all burn up too?

I knew we were losing altitude. My ears had plugged, and I forced a yawn to open them. Outside the window the sun was touching the western horizon, the plane was banking, turning, sunlight moving across the fuselage to the opposite wall, and we were not going to Albuquerque any more.

Suddenly there was nothing to be done. No more going or becoming, nothing left to think, only a silence within and throughout the shuddering cabin. *Peace, be still. All shall be well, and all manner of thing shall be well.*

How long was it, then, before I noticed people speaking quietly to each other again? The cabin still shook, the flight attendants remained in their quarters where they had withdrawn. My ears plugged once more; I yawned again to open them.

When the captain came back on the intercom he sounded in command as before. "Ladies and gentlemen, we've encountered a problem with an engine and have decided to return to Salt Lake where our technicians can check it. We expect to land in about ten minutes. As a standard precaution, we've arranged for emergency vehicles to be on hand. Please follow the crew's instructions for your comfort and safety, and when our mechanics have had a look we'll get you flying to Albuquerque again as soon as possible."

My seatmate wondered aloud what else a pilot could say to souls in his safekeeping, and I asked what the captain knew that could not be said.

We approached the city, saw the airfield ahead and below. The ground kept rising to meet us. As the wheels touched down and we rolled along the runway the flashing lights of ambulances, fire trucks, and police cars were a blur of colours on the darkening desert sky. The plane slowed and the shuddering eased, we trundled to the terminal and disembarked — safe, for the moment, and sound.

For an hour we waited in the airport. Some of us talked over a coffee until both our anxiety and its relief were past. Eventually an announcement came that a replacement aircraft was on the way, and we could probably reboard the flight within the next hour.

When we were finally airborne again, the captain spoke early on, thanking us for our patience. He reported that one engine of the ailing plane had caught fire. Though there'd been some apprehensive moments, it turned out that we hadn't been in any great danger, for the blaze had burned itself out before we landed. He promised the flight deck would put on extra speed and have us in Albuquerque as quickly as they could. Meanwhile, the crew would serve champagne and sandwiches in token of the airline's thanks.

The rest of the trip passed festively. That night when we landed I took a cab to a hotel, and next morning boarded a bus which indeed turned left at Albuquerque and drove up to Santa Fe and to the Pecos desert cloister beyond with its adobe walls shining in the autumn sun.

That week for me was the total immersion of a lapsed Mennonite into a wide community of souls. We listened to our mentors. In one lecture Morton Kelsey held up a Bible from which he'd cut out all the dreams and visionary material, flexed the scissored pages and said that now it was a hole-y book indeed. Many newfound friends held spirited discussions, each day I took solitary walks in the desert, and at night the moon was reflected in a still pond beside the chapel. The retreat, alas, was over too soon.

On the return flight, our plane bounced more than flew through turbulent weather all the way back to Salt Lake City. But the engines never faltered, and the cabin held tight. From there, up to Calgary and a short hop over to Saskatoon, and one more taxi ride back to my apartment.

Inside, I glanced at the week's mail, and opened my luggage to unpack. One suitcase was full of books I'd bought in New Mexico. But I had also tucked a shampoo bottle between them, which in the high altitude had popped open and soaked, stained, and warped every one of the new volumes. As if to serve notice that life will not be gained by searching Jungian scriptures either, that it lies up yonder after all, where there's nothing to do but let be.

☾

Acknowledgements

Many of the quotations and allusions in *Bindy's Moon* are in the public domain. The following references are cited with gratitude:

The epigraph by N. Scott Momaday is taken from *The Way to Rainy Mountain* (University of New Mexico Press, 1969).

The "Horizon Prayer" on page 71 is from a poem by Rossiter W. Raymond, more recently transcribed into a song by Carly Simon.

Mel Blanc's witticism on page 92 appears in his autobiography co-written with Philip Bashe, *That's Not All, Folks!* (Warner Books, 1989).

The anecdote of the abbot and the monks on page 101 and 102 is in Nikos Kazantzakis, *The Last Temptation of Christ* (Faber & Faber, 1988).

Edwin Arlington Robinson's phrase on page 109 is from "The Valley of the Shadow" in *Three Taverns: a book of poems* (Macmillan, 1922).

The quotation on page 121 is from "An Old Man's Winter Night" in Robert Frost's *The Poems of Robert Frost* (Washington Square Press, 1967).

The lines from Teilhard de Chardin on page 127 appear in *The Prayer of the Universe* (Fontana, 1973).

I'm more than thankful to:

Thistledown Press for this third support of my writing.

The Saskatchewan Writers Guild for retreats, manuscript evaluation services, and the honour of a John V. Hicks Long Manuscript Award for *Bindy's Moon*.

The Saskatchewan Arts Board for an Independent Artist grant.

Friends who read rough and unready drafts and offered comments: Glen Sorestad, Rita Bouvier, Gerry Hill, Seán Virgo, Jeff Ratzlaff, and my daughters Shannon Kutcher and Sheri Porrelli.

Editors who published early versions of some parts of the book in *Rhubarb, NeWest Review, Journal of Mennonite Studies, Dream Network: A Journal Exploring Dreams and Myth*, and *Saskatchewan Writers: Lives Past and Present*.

I'm especially indebted to the editors of *Prairie Messenger Catholic Journal*: Maureen Weber for giving me fifteen years of free exploration in a monthly column; Donald Ward who so congenially also edited *Bindy's Moon*; and Abbot Peter Novecosky who continues to offer Benedictine hospitality to many writers at St. Peter's Abbey in Muenster, Saskatchewan.

And finally, Larraine as always for the levity and love that raise me from what I was.

Bindy's Moon is the third book in Lloyd Ratzlaff's series of literary essays. Ratzlaff is also the editor of an anthology of seniors' writings published by READ Saskatoon and a columnist for the *Prairie Messenger Catholic Journal*. He has served on the boards of several writing organizations and taught writing classes for the University of Saskatchewan Certificate of Art & Design program and the Western Development Museum. Ratzlaff lives in Saskatoon.